JONATHAN
EDWARDS

☆

The GREAT AMERICAN THINKERS *Series*

JONATHAN EDWARDS

Alfred Owen Aldridge, Ph.D.
Head of the Department of Comparative Literature
University of Maryland

SERIES EDITORS
Arthur W. Brown, Ph.D.
President, Adelphi University; and

Thomas S. Knight, Ph.D.
Professor and Chairman of the
Department of Philosophy, Adelphi University

WSP
∏

WASHINGTON SQUARE PRESS, INC. • NEW YORK • 1966

PREFACE

In this study of Jonathan Edwards I have emphasized certain features of his life which previous biographers have passed over, and in attempting to relate his philosophy to the prevailing notions of his age, I may have exposed some unorthodox perspectives. But in the exposition of every point I have relied on Edwards' own words rather than on the schools of opinion which have grown up around him.

I am grateful to the General Research Board of the University of Maryland for a grant which helped to make the writing of this book possible.

CONTENTS

☆

JONATHAN
EDWARDS

Chapter 1

THE LIFE: MAN OF GOD

For most people Jonathan Edwards is merely a quiet Puritan who in his youth studied spiders and stumbled onto a system of philosophical idealism, who followed his ancestors into the pulpit but lost the good will of his flock by tenaciously clinging to old-fashioned doctrine, and who wrote an encyclopedic defense of the Calvinistic concept of determinism. This is the bare outline of Edwards' life, and superficially there is very little to add except, of course, the chronicle of births, marriages, and deaths in his domestic circle and the bibliography of his sermons and theological controversies. Yet a modern poet, Robert Lowell, has woven the drab materials of this uneventful life into a compelling biographical poem, "Mr. Edwards and the Spider." Other people, repelled by Edwards' austere doctrine, have similarly been fascinated by the mystery of how a philosopher of any eminence at all could have sprung from the provincial intellectual milieu of New England in the first decade of the eighteenth century.

Benjamin Franklin, only three years Edwards' junior, whose life presents intriguing parallels and contrasts, rose from essentially the same environment but escaped at an early age to a more cosmopolitan atmosphere.

Jonathan Edwards was born October 5, 1703, in a literal wilderness: at East Windsor, Connecticut, then a remote frontier village. He came of sturdy stock: his mother lived to the age of ninety; his father, to eighty-nine, dying only two months before his son. Jonathan was the only boy among ten sisters. Both his grandfather and his father were ministers, and his solid and abiding heritage was the Bible and New England theology. About all he seems to have drawn from his frontier environment was an acute sensitivity to nature.

We know a good deal about Edwards' boyhood, thanks to his "Personal Narrative," written when he was about thirty-six, a document as revealing in its way as Franklin's autobiography. At the age of five or six he had his first religious experience, concomitant with "a time of remarkable awakening" among his father's congregation. This led him to a concern for his soul's salvation and with the outward duties of religion. He "used to pray five times a day in secret, and to spend much time in religious conversation with other boys." So great was his delight in "religious duties" that he joined with his schoolmates "and built a booth in a swamp in a very retired spot, for a place of prayer." Franklin at about the same time of life was leading his playmates in building a fishing wharf in a salt marsh, stealing for the purpose a heap of stones intended for the building of a house. He received a paternal rebuke for his enterprise, despite its utility, on the grounds that "nothing was useful which was not honest." Edwards' rebuke was self-administered. He later disparaged his own precocious piety on the grounds that a delight in religion should never be mistaken for grace—as though he felt guilty for having found pleasure in his pious inclinations.

Although Edwards sought to minimize the importance of his early experience—and a later critic has expressed it as "playing religion"—his emotional state then was not very different from the condition which Edwards in later life described as "conversion." Indeed shortly after a frenzied revival during his own ministry, he made a good deal of the emotional transfiguration of a four-year-old girl, which he recognized as a genuine conversion. Among Christians of Edwards' stamp, it was almost a behavior pattern to doubt one's conversion and to require a confirming or superseding experience. There was a continuous development from Edwards' boyhood playing at religion to his "delightful conviction" of God's absolute sovereignty in his maturity.

Another pattern among evangelical Christians was to exaggerate the heinousness of the sins of which they were allegedly guilty. John Bunyan felt that he was the "chief of sinners" because he liked to ring the bells and play tip cat on Sunday. Edwards never specified the nature of the "old ways of sin" into which he supposedly slipped back after a seizure of pleurisy, but his "wicked ways" were probably no more serious than Bunyan's.

According to Edwards' grandson, who first collected Edwards' papers, his earliest composition, written at about the age of ten, was a satirical attack on the notion that the human soul is material and remains with the body until resurrection. A single paragraph, it is one of the most stylistically successful pieces Edwards ever wrote. Unfortunately he never fully developed the vein of irony it contains, which varies from facetious quips to caustic aspersions. Supposing that the soul is material, Edwards asked whether it remains within the body at death and, if so, whether the coffin needs a special repository to house it. The coffin-maker would need to know "what Shape it is of, whether round, triangular or foresquare, or whether it is a number of long fine strings reaching from head to foot, and whether it does not live a very discontented life."

Edwards subsequently wrote thousands of pages of prose, but his style never improved. The importance of this piece is in the evidence it offers of Edwards' early opposition to materialism. His famous idealism was a natural second step, perhaps not even requiring the additional stimulus of reading the theories of other philosophers.

His earliest dated letter which has survived is addressed to one of his sisters (May 10, 1716) and describes a record number of conversions under his father's ministry. Young Edwards outlined the number of adhesions to the church and of those who periodically conversed with his father about their souls in much the same manner in which a twelve-year-old in our society might describe the season record of a winning football team. The "remarkable outpouring of the Spirit of God" which he recorded was a recurrent phenomenon in the church of the time, culminating in the Great Awakening of Edwards' maturity.

Edwards' essay entitled "Of Insects," which deals exclusively with spiders, is usually thought to have been written at about the same time, since he speaks of himself as "a Child" in a covering letter communicating the essay to someone in the "Learned World." Yet in the text itself he refers to remembrances of "when I was a boy," indicating that the essay as it now exists may have been a later revision of an earlier effort. Also it shows a great knowledge of the laws of hydraulics as applied to swimming, which it is hard to believe Edwards could have acquired by experience alone. As a boy, he may very well have lain on the ground upon his back observing spiders, but there is no evidence that he then knew about the forces which will carry a man from the bottom of the sea "if he has hold on a stick of wood or anything that is lighter or takes up more space for the quantity of matter than the water." Although Yale's Benjamin Silliman remarked in the *American Journal of Science and Arts* that the subject of spiders "examined, so sagaciously . . . , by the philosophical child, remains nearly as he left it," Edwards treatment was patently fragmentary. He limited his discussion to the spiders' method of locomotion—their "swimming" or "marching" in the air from tree to tree—and said nothing whatsoever about such important matters as their diet or breeding habits. By repeated observation he discovered that the spiders "put out a web at their tails," which, being lighter than air, enables them to ascend or descend at will and travel in currents of air. Spiders let out their webs, the young scientist conjectured, not only to stay alive but also to enjoy "a Great Deal of their sort of Pleasure." Edwards viewed the universe in much the same light as Addison did in his famous *Spectator* paper in which he elucidated the final causes of the pleasures of imagination (No. 413). According to the *Spectator*, God "has made every thing that is beautiful in our own species pleasant, that all creatures might be tempted to multiply their kind, and fill the world with inhabitants." Edwards pointed to "the exuberant goodness of the Creator who hath not only provided for all the necessities but also for the pleasure and recreation of all sorts of creatures. And even the insects and those that are most despicable." Edwards discerned another final cause of the pleasure which spiders found in flying: to bring about their final destruction and prevent an overpopulation of insects. He believed that, in the fall of the year, they are attracted into the air by sunshine and driven by the prevailing winds out to sea and drowned—a hypothesis certainly not accepted by present-day entomologists. But for Edwards it was reason to "behold and admire at the wisdom of the Creator and be convinced from Providence . . . [of the] wonderful contrivance of annually carrying off and burying the corrupting nauseousness of our air, of which flying insects are little collections in the bottom of ocean."

The voice was that of a scientist, but the hand was that of a theologian. Yet there is no doubt that Edwards in his youth, perhaps even more than in later periods of his life, felt a direct and sensual pleasure in the beauties of nature. He enjoyed looking through the dazzling rays of the sun, sheltering his eyes with his hand, at the "multitudes of little shining webbs and glistening strings of a great length" made by the spiders. On other sunny days, he would squirt water from his mouth to form his own rainbows and revel in the array of colors. His later manner of characterizing spiritual experiences drew upon his delight in nature. Holiness, to him, resembled "a field or garden of God, with all manner of pleasant flowers; enjoying a sweet calm, and the gentle vivifying beams of the sun." Then the soul "appeared like such a little white flower as we see in the spring of the year; low and humble on the ground, opening its bosom to receive the pleasant beams of the sun's glory." At the age of forty, he compared a religious experience to the change of seasons, contemplating the manner in which "God may bring on a spiritual spring as he does the natural, with now and then a pleasant sunshiny season, and then an interruption by clouds and stormy winds, till at length, by the sun more and more approaching, and the light increasing, the strength of winter is broken."

The theological doctrine which gave Edwards the greatest comfort and even delight throughout his life was that of God's absolute sovereignty in the universe. He felt a firm conviction of the rightness of things akin to that of the deists. The prevailing temper of the age—Christian or deistical—based on either Newton or the Scriptures—held that God was perfect and benevolent and that the universe, under divine supervision, was orderly, controlled, and equally salutary for all creatures.

According to Edwards' "Personal Narrative," he first experienced his "inward, sweet delight in God and divine things" in reading a verse in I Timothy: "Now unto the King eternal, immortal, invisible, the only wise God, be honour and glory for ever and ever. Amen." Of all the verses in the New Testament, this is among the most formal and perfunctory. Edwards' sentiment must have been already in existence, although a single word or concept in this particular passage may have sparked the explosion of his fervor. Perhaps for the first time he considered the philosophical significance of such concepts as eternity, immortality, or wisdom. Or perhaps the phrase "the only wise God" suggested to him the superiority of his own insights and theology and pointed to his favorite notion of the absolute sovereignty of God. From about this time Edwards came to have "pleasant views and contemplations" of the doctrines which had been instilled into him from birth, and he spent his time reading and meditating on the "beauty and excellency" of Christ.

His favorite reading was the Book of Canticles, which gave him an "inward sweetness" or a "calm, sweet abstraction of soul from all the concerns of the world." At other times he had "a kind of vision, or fixed ideas and imaginations, of being alone in the mountains, or some solitary wilderness, far from all mankind, sweetly conversing with Christ, and wrapt and swallowed up in God." His "sense of divine things" came upon him in flashes, creating "a sweet harmony" or ardor in his heart. Although lacking words to give precise expression to his feelings, he confided them to his father and received paternal and pastoral encouragement. After unburdening himself, he walked alone in his father's pasture, contemplating the sky and clouds. There came upon him a feeling of real rapture, "a sense of the glorious *majesty* and *grace* of God," qualities which he seemed to visualize in "a sweet conjunction" of gentle majesty and majestic meekness. The young man's ecstasy was so extensive that God's wisdom, purity, and excellence seemed to shine forth in all parts of nature—from the grass and trees to the planets and stars. Even thunderstorms, which formerly had terrified him, became a symbol of the presence of God. Rejoicing at the signs of their imminence, he placed himself in a convenient position "to view the clouds, and see the lightnings play, and hear the majestic and awful voice of God's thunders, which oftentimes was exceedingly entertaining." At other times, Edwards engaged in almost constant singing and ejaculatory prayer.

As the son of a minister, Edwards was given a sound training in the fundamentals of classical learning, and his intellectual progress kept pace with his spiritual development. He began studying Latin at the age of six and then advanced to Greek and Hebrew. Yet we have no evidence to place Edwards in the category of intellectual precociousness exhibited by such prodigies as Godwin or John Stuart Mill, who wrote copiously in the classical languages at the age of seven or eight and were masters of several modern tongues. Even as a grown man Edwards did not stand out in his century for learning. He acquired an extensive knowledge of the Scriptures, Calvinistic theology, and some philosophical writers in the Christian tradition, but there were many areas, including literature and history, with which he lacked even an elementary acquaintance. He never learned a single modern language and later regretted that he could not read the theological works in French which some of his Scottish friends sent him.

A month before his thirteenth birthday, Edwards was enrolled at Yale College. Since there were no high schools in those days, this was the normal age. Candidates for the ministry were admitted as soon as they had mastered the curriculum of the village schools: arithmetic, algebra, geometry, mathematics, and one or more classical languages, depending on the capacities of the schoolmaster. The first two years of college offered little but an extension of these subjects together with logic and a great deal of Bible reading.

When Edwards enrolled at Yale, in the fall of 1716, the fledgling institution was in the throes of a turbulence which threatened to destroy it altogether. Although the first student had enrolled in 1702, and the first degree had been granted in the same year, the institution had no fixed residence when Edwards entered. Some of the tutors with their students functioned at New Haven. Others carried on with equal prestige and authority at Saybrook and Wethersfield. But a stroke of good fortune for the college made it necessary to decide on a permanent location—the arrival from London of two collections of books, totaling one thousand volumes. The trustees decided in November that henceforth Yale should be confined to New Haven and appointed a new tutor, Samuel Johnson, later to be president of King's College. The freshman class of ten students started out the year in New Haven, but for some still unexplained reason decamped a few weeks later to Wethersfield—ten miles from Edwards' home at East

[7]

Windsor. Their self-chosen tutor was Elisha Williams, Edwards' cousin from an affluent branch of the family, eventually to declare itself hostile toward Edwards.

Perhaps under the influence of the dissensions of the Yale tutors and trustees (in 1718 separate commencement exercises were held in Wethersfield and New Haven), Edwards' religious dedication dimmed somewhat. He wrote one relatively long letter to his sister Mary, including absolutely no mention of God or providence, one of the few documents, of similar length in his career with such an omission. Hurt because he had not heard "one tittle" from his sister and disappointed that there should be no correspondence between them, he gave her an account of school politics, reporting the decision of all factions to return to New Haven and to replace Samuel Johnson with Timothy Cutler as Rector.

This is the period during which Edwards became acquainted with Locke's *Essay Concerning Human Understanding*, an intellectual adventure which may have momentarily diverted his attention from things divine to things human. He later confided that at the age of fourteen he had discovered more delight in reading Locke "than the most greedy miser finds, when gathering up handfuls of silver and gold, from some newly discovered treasure."

While studying Locke, Edwards compiled a series of original notes on fundamental metaphysical problems, using Locke's epistemological approach to arrive at his solutions. Even his proof for the existence of God is essentially an elaboration of Locke: Absolute nothing is an impossibility; therefore there must be an eternal being, something which existed before the creation of the universe; and this omnipresent being is God. Only atheists could accept a universe which had always existed. As pure logic, Edwards' reasoning is an improvement over Locke, who started with the premise that since man has perception and knowledge, there has always been a knowing, intelligent being in the world. Locke, like Descartes, reasons from the self to the universe; Edwards starts with existence *per se* and goes directly to God. Unconsciously venturing into poetry, Edwards suggested that, to form an idea of nothing, "we must think of the same that the sleeping Rocks dream of."

From his proof of the existence of God Edwards derived

a modified form of idealism based on the hypothesis that there can be no existence without consciousness. Our world, he argued, has no existence beyond that in the consciousness of each of its inhabitants as well as in the consciousness of God. In buttressing his theory, Edwards formulated one of the major doctrines of his later treatise on the will—that there is a chain of cause and effect uniting all activity in the universe. If we imagine a tightly shut room, the contents of which nobody but God can see or hear, we must not conclude, according to Edwards' theory of idealism, that this room does not exist for created beings, "for perhaps there is not one leaf of a tree nor spire of grass but what has effects all over the universe and will have to the end of eternity." Nevertheless Edwards insisted that one cannot suppose a universe of order and harmony, containing nothing but senseless bodies, for such a world could have being only in divine consciousness and in no other form. If for a certain span of time all minds or spirits, including God's, were deprived of consciousness, "the universe for that time would cease to be of itself."

Edwards impugned the intellectual processes of those who would not accept his theory. It is only our imagination, he charged, which makes us believe that shapes and magnitudes could exist without someone to behold them, but our imagination is deceptive. Since his entire theory of idealism grew out of the alleged deceptiveness of sense perceptions, Edwards presumably accepted nothing but reason and intuition as his insight into reality.

Various thinkers, including Berkeley, have been suggested as possible sources for Edwards' conclusion that the world is an ideal one, but chronology invalidates the supposition that Edwards knew the Irish bishop. Since Locke and Newton are the only modern philosophers we can be absolutely sure that Edwards read at this time, the probability is that Edwards reached his idealism independently. He himself once pointed out that his ideas could be the same as those of a writer whom he had not read. Referring to the similarity between his views on communion and those of Isaac Watts, he affirmed that he had not seen Watts's book when he published his own ideas. "But yet I think," he wrote, "my sentiments, as I have expressed them, are as exactly agreeable to what he lays down, as if I had been his pupil."

Edwards' philosophical speculation went hand in hand with his college courses in physics, "natural philosophy," divinity, and ethics, which graced the curriculum of the third and fourth years. As part of his independent study, Edwards set forth his thoughts in copious "Remarks and Reflections of a Religious Nature" and "Notes on the Scriptures." The latter, which he extended during his ministry, was designed to be an encyclopedic attempt to answer every objection to the Scriptures and explain every difficulty, not "by disguising or misstating them, but by giving them their full force, and meeting them with fair argument." Typical problems were the sacrifice of Jephthah's daughter (she was not put to death but dedicated to perpetual virginity) and the sun's standing still for Joshua (the sun actually remained in a fixed position for twenty-four hours and scorched the earth in some places, giving rise to the Greek myth of Phaeton).

The college year in those days began and ended in September, and Edwards completed his studies in 1720, just before his seventeenth birthday. As the highest ranking scholar of his class, he recited the Latin valedictory oration. But the farewell was merely symbolic, since Edwards stayed on at Yale for two years of graduate divinity studies.

Even in the days when most college students were preparing for the ministry and attended to their responsibilities with grim dedication, Edwards stood out for his soberness and austerity. For this reason he was given in the college dining hall or "buttery" the important post of "butler," requiring him to apportion equal servings of the day's menu to his classmates. As a graduate student, he shared a room with his cousin Elisha Mix, a freshman who resented Edwards' enforcement of a custom by which older students exacted certain services of the lower classmen. When the boys foolishly took their quarrels to their parents, Edwards' father, Timothy, instead of telling his son to fight his own battles, wrote to the Mixes, complaining not only of Elisha's lack of respect for Jonathan, but of Elisha's mother having talked about Jonathan before three young women in a manner tending "not a little to diminish him and blemish his name." This was the first of a series of family quarrels which were to plague Edwards' entire career. Probably his sense of his own rectitude coupled with his respect for authority led him as a student to appeal to the family elders. He would have done better to wonder whether anything inherent in his personality kept him from getting along with his cousin.

Apparently Edwards realized that he was deficient in social inclinations, for he wrote to his father shortly after the incident, "I am much reformed with respect to visiting of friends, and intend to do more at it for the future than in time past" (March 1, 1721). Later as a minister he recognized that he was remiss in making pastoral rounds, but vindicated himself by minimizing their importance to the clerical calling.

Edwards' sympathies were automatically drawn to the side of authority. When the undergraduates characteristically protested against the quality of the college food by boycotting the commons, Edwards immediately rebuked one of his acquaintances so sternly that the rebel acutely regretted his insubordination. Edwards wrote to his father that in his opinion "there has been very little occasion for such an insurrection as this." His complacence may have been in part due to the fact that he never took any great pleasure in eating. Withdrawn from most of his fellow students, Edwards wrote with satisfaction, "I live in very good amity and agreement with my chambermate—there has no new quarrel broke out betwixt me and any of the scholars," giving the impression that it was only rarely that this harmony existed. He stood on the sidelines viewing the "monstrous impieties and acts of immorality" committed by his classmates—"particularly stealing of hens, geese, turkeys, pigs, meat, wood, &c.—unseasonable nightwalking, breaking people's windows, playing at cards, cursing, swearing, and damning, and using all manner of ill language." Smugly or not, Edwards rejoiced that he was "perfectly free of all their janglings."

Some time during his Yale period, Edwards had the experience which he considered his authentic conversion, one of the most vague and cloudy episodes of his life. Even in his "Personal Narrative," he described it only obliquely—revealing merely that it had brought him to "new dispositions" and a "new sense of things." Certainly his first realization of religious conviction did not seem to conform to the experiences of others he wrote about in his theological works, a circumstance which frequently troubled him. It has been said that Edwards "first endeavored to search out the innerness of the experience and to understand it himself; then he endeavored to translate it into doctrine." More realistically, he first accepted the doctrine ready made almost by a process of osmosis and then worked himself into an emotional experience to render it sublime. His careful attempt to distinguish between the external piety of his boyhood and the inner conviction of his youth fails to show a concrete difference in kind. Essentially all he could say in his "Personal Narrative" was that "those former delights never reached the heart; and did not arise from any sight of the divine excellency of the things of God; or any taste of the soul-satisfying and life-giving good there is in them." In his diary (December, 1722) he gave four reasons for questioning his "interest in God's love and favor": He could not be sure of having experienced "that preparatory work, of which divines speak"; he had not "experienced regeneration, exactly in those steps in which divines say it is generally wrought"; he did not feel the Christian graces sensibly enough, particularly faith, fearing that his religious feelings were "only such hypocritical outside affections, which wicked men may feel as well as others"; and he was sometimes guilty of sins of omission and commission, particularly of evil speaking. In the following month, he renewed his baptismal covenant, affirming, "I have been before God, and have given myself, all that I am and have, to God." But, over two years later, he was still not certain of the genuineness of his conversion.

There was nothing unusual in Edwards' doubting the validity of a first conversion and seeking the exaltation of a subsequent emotional feeling. His wife and daughters went through the same pattern of undergoing a second revitalizing experience. And Watts held as doctrine that the Christian first attains salvation (the "first witness") and then subsequently receives an internal assurance (the "second witness").

Paradoxically, Edwards underwent the emotional regeneration which dedicated him with renewed fervor to Calvinism at about the moment when his preceptors were abandoning both Calvinism and emotional religion. In the fall of 1722, the rector of Yale College, Timothy Cutler, and two of his tutors boldly announced their conversion to the Anglican faith and declared that the method of ordination by other ministers instead of bishops was invalid. Edwards makes no allusion to

this apostasy in any of his surviving writings, but the precocious Franklin used the event as a topical allusion to advance
the theme that "there are too many blind zealots among every
denomination of Christians." In the wake of the betrayal of
puritan orthodoxy at Yale, the trustees declared that henceforth every faculty member must declare his acceptance of
the Saybrook platform (congregational principles of church
government united with the doctrine of the Westminster Confession), a requirement with which Edwards unhesitatingly
complied when he himself became a Yale tutor. Had he ever
been in danger of any deviation from absolute Calvinism, he
thereby became officially wedded to it.

In August, 1722, Edwards became minister of a small Presbyterian congregation in New York—a splinter group of Eng-
lishmen who had broken away from the church of a Scots-
man, James Anderson, because they could not endure his
Scottish brogue and peculiarities. The atmosphere of New
York, where Edwards continued for eight months, seems to
have wrought no change whatsoever upon his outlook, his
interests being limited to his devotions, his studies, and his
small congregation. According to the scant evidence available, he seems to have formed only one solid and lasting
friendship at this time. It was with the son of his landlady,
a certain John Smith, probably part of the family of one of
the church trustees, Thomas Smith, whom Edwards regarded
as a person of uncommon piety and purity and with whom
he engaged in Bible reading and religious conversation.

This is probably the period, referred to in one of his treatises, when he lived next door to a Jew, whose dedication filled
him with awe. Edwards considered his neighbor to be the
most reverent person he had ever seen, much of his time being spent in acts of devotion at his eastern window, not only
in the daytime but sometimes during whole nights.

While in New York, Edwards formed a series of thirty-four
resolutions concerning the regulation of his spiritual life,
which he later brought up to the number of seventy. The
adopting of such resolutions was common at the time—by no
means limited to candidates for the ministry. Benjamin Franklin followed the same procedure in his efforts to attain moral
perfection by defining thirteen virtues in a small notebook
and checking off all infractions. Franklin also inculcated the

social virtues by joining with a group of other young men to discuss ethical problems and to initiate reforms and useful projects.

Edwards' resolutions covered both personal and social ethics:

1. *Resolved*, That *I will do whatsoever* I think to be most to the glory of God, and my own good, profit, and pleasure, in the whole of my duration; without any consideration of the time, whether now, or never so many myriads of ages hence. *Resolved*, to do whatever I think to be my *duty*, and most for the good and advantage of mankind in general. *Resolved*, so to do, whatever *difficulties* I meet with, how many soever, and how great soever.

2. *Resolved*, To be continually endeavouring to find out some *new contrivance* and invention to promote the fore-mentioned things.

. . . .

13. *Resolved*, To be endeavouring to find out fit objects of liberality and charity.

But the individual emphasis of the Calvinist theology triumphed over the social impulse, and Edwards arrived at a type of guilt-conscious categorical imperative.

8. *Resolved*, To act in all respects, both speaking and doing, as if nobody had been so vile as I, and as if I had committed the same sins, or had the same infirmities or failings, as others; and that I will let the knowledge of their failings promote nothing but shame in myself, and prove only an occasion of my confessing my own sins and misery to God.

Like most rigorous Calvinists, Edwards was not aware of the dichotomy in his social and theological attitudes—on the one hand holding himself self-righteously aloof from the pranks of the other boys at Yale and on the other condemning himself as the blackest of sinners.

Even though his theology kept him from seeking to attain moral perfection in the optimistic or presumptuous manner of Franklin, Edwards nevertheless made the supposition that there could be but one individual "who was properly a complete Christian," and he resolved to "act just as I would do, if I strove with all my might to be that one."

Naturally, for Edwards, religion was paramount in his resolutions as well as in his life.

44. *Resolved*, That no other end but religion shall have any influence at all on any of my actions; and that no action shall be, in the least circumstance, any otherwise than the religious end will carry it.

45. *Resolved*, Never to allow any pleasure or grief, joy or sorrow, nor any affection at all, nor any degree of affection, nor any circumstance relating to it, but what helps religion.

Besides his resolutions, Edwards entered into his notebooks a collection of original emblems or observations of allegorical resemblances between nature and his religious system. Looking for emblems was an old pastime for Puritans, indeed part and parcel of their religious belief. Originally these emblems noted resemblances between an Old Testament forerunner (the type) and a New Testament successor (the antitype). Adam was a type, for example, and Christ, "the second Adam," an antitype. Jonah's three-day descent into the internal regions of the whale was a type or emblem of Christ's burial. Eventually typology got out of hand as zealous expositors produced metaphors so elaborate and fanciful that they came to resemble the ingenious conceits of the metaphysical poets rather than the earnest moralizing of John Bunyan's *Pilgrim's Progress*. Most devisers of emblems were engaging in pious exercises or intellectual games, but for Edwards the method represented a serious philosophical pursuit, a highroad to metaphysical truth. As we shall see later, he actually believed that God found pleasure in analogies, and that by discovering those which God has implanted in nature we can penetrate into the secrets of being. We shall also see that Edwards embodied his emblematic epistemology in one of his most serious philosophical works, his treatise on "The Nature of True Virtue."

Edwards' emblems have been published under the title

[15]

Images or Shadows of Divine Things, but he also called them *The Book of Nature and Common Providence and The Language and Lessons of Nature.* In one of his most commonplace emblems, Edwards declared, "The rising and setting of the sun is a type of the death and resurrection of Christ" (No. 50). In another, more individual, he expounded the *raison d'être* of the method of typology:

> . . . It is apparent and allowed that there is a great and remarkable analogy in God's works. There is a wonderfull [sic] resemblance in the effects which God produces, and consentaneity in His manner of working in one thing and another throughout all nature. It is very observable in the visible world; therefore it is allowed that God does purposely make and order one thing to be in agreeableness and harmony with another. And if so, why should we not suppose that He makes the inferiour in imitation of the superiour, the material of the spiritual, on purpose to have a resemblance and shadow of them? We see that even in the material world, God makes one part of it strangely to agree with another, and why is it not reasonable to suppose He makes the whole as a shadow of the spiritual world? (No. 8)

In May 1723, Edwards took leave of his New York parishioners, his heart seeming to sink within him "at leaving the family and city" where he had "enjoyed so many sweet and pleasant days." After a summer with his parents, Edwards returned to New Haven in the fall for independent study, receiving the M.A. degree in September. Very little trace of his external activities in these days has remained, but we may follow his inner life through his diary.

In a spirit of extreme asceticism he declared his intention "to live in continual mortification, without ceasing, and even to weary myself thereby, as long as I am in this world, and never to expect or desire any worldly ease or pleasure" (Jan. 6, 1723). Yet on another day he admitted that some delights or satisfactions not connected with a religious end might still have validity—otherwise we should never rejoice at the sight of friends; and if we had no pleasure in food, our health would be impaired (Jan. 12, 1723). Edwards used his diary as a commentary on his resolutions and a record of the degree to which he adhered to them. According to his theology, these resolutions were of absolutely no avail without the grace of God. The strength of human character counted for nothing. Curiously, however, he assumed that he was himself to blame for negligence and failure (Jan. 2 & 5, 1723). Similarly, according to this strange logic, Edwards felt that he must not admit any praise for the good he might do, but must accept all the blame for any evil (Jan. 12, 1723). His afflictions came upon him, he believed, as corrections for sin, but there was no place in his theology for virtue to receive any reward (Jan. 2, 1723). This is the vein of one of his sermons, in which he preached that men can reject Christ, but they cannot accept him.

Despite this lopsided equity, Edwards conformed to the spirit of the age by affirming "a universal benevolence and good nature" (Aug. 9, 1723). In regard to the practical affairs of life, he advocated dwelling on the bright side of things (Nov. 26, 1723), and those religious doctrines which we may judge grim and somber, he considered cheery and bright. His favorite doctrines were those of "election, free grace, our inability to do any thing without the grace of God," and, one particularly Edwardsian, that "holiness is entirely, throughout, the work of the Spirit of God." At the age of twenty Edwards had thus organized in capsule form the theology of his lifetime. In essence, it was traditional Calvinism modified by new doctrines of affection and benevolence. It could be summarized as gloomy optimism. Edwards was to go through no mental crises, ascend through no further stages of development. His intellectual horizon was exactly the same when he died as when he was a young divinity student.

Edwards loaded his diary with references to his sins in general and to his repentance for them, but the only one he particularly specified was evil speaking—and this he mentioned repeatedly, evidence perhaps that he was somewhat undecided about the true nature of his rigorous denunciation of other people's frailties (July 20, 1723). Indeed, from his collection of emblems we gather that Edwards considered that his most grave weaknesses in daily living consisted in his overindulging temper and sex. "There is the tongue," he wrote, "and another member of the body that have a natural

[17]

bridle, which is to signify to us the peculiar need we have to bridle and restrain those two members." (The bridle of the tongue—hardly obvious—consists of "the double row of teeth.") Edwards admitted also as a personal defect that he found it difficult to trust God and keep faith when he was convinced in advance that an event would be adverse (July 29, 1723). At times when he was violently beset with temptation or evil thoughts he applied himself to mathematics in order to keep his mind engaged (July 27, 1723).

Almost the only nonreligious information which Edwards included in his diary is the fact that when he was in New York and meditated on religion, he used to imagine himself as walking in the fields at home, but when he returned home, he imagined himself as walking in the fields at New York (May 2, 1724). Anticipating a fundamental doctrine of Freudian psychology, he analyzed his dreams every morning as soon as he awoke, establishing "the nature, circumstance, principles, and ends of my imaginary actions and passions in them; in order to discern what are my prevailing inclinations." He also felt that his disposition was most lively and cheerful on the days when he had read the Scriptures most (May 23, 1724).

Edwards continued independent study and occasional supply work at New Haven until June, 1724, when he was appointed one of three tutors at Yale. Because of the Cutler scandal, the college had had no official head for four years, and the tutors were virtually in control. Very shortly they restored the institution to its previous orthodox regularity. In the first week of his new duties, Edwards confided to his diary, "I have now abundant reason to be convinced of the troublesomeness and vexation of the world, and that it will never be another kind of world." Probably this is another indication of his poor adjustment to social life. The crosses he met with in the subsequent week thrust him "quite below all comforts in religion" (Sept. 12, 1724). His only resource was in a "far stronger and more permanent faith, hope, and love." Gentleness, he felt, was the virtue which he needed to impart "a beauty and lustre" to his behavior (Feb. 16, 1725). To keep himself from the temptation of too much sleeping, he naïvely looked for a type analogy and concluded that "Christ has recommended rising early in the morning, by his rising from the grave very early" (Jan., 1728).

Although both of Edwards' parents were sturdy, vigorous people, and Edwards' own height of six feet one inch gave him an imposing appearance, his constitution was always frail. In 1725 he suffered a severe illness, lasting three months, and he never regained the strength and vitality of his younger days.

His grandfather, Solomon Stoddard, then eighty-two years old, was still carrying on the duties of pastor of the Northampton, Massachusetts, congregation, the most important in the colony outside of Boston. Having served without interruption since 1672, Stoddard had become almost a legend in ministerial circles. His great theological innovation had been the practice of admitting to the sacrament of the Lord's Supper any persons of good character, instead of limiting it to those who could attest to a definite experience of conversion. By considering the sacrament as a "converting ordinance," Stoddard liberalized the conditions of church membership (a religious-civic duality) in much the same way that the Whigs in England were extending political privileges through the device of "occasional conformity."

Soon after Edwards was restored to health, the Northampton congregation invited him to become the venerable Stoddard's associate and eventual successor, and on February 15, 1727, he officially entered upon his duties. Five months later he married. His bride, Sarah Pierrepont, was as well suited to his temperament and background as was his grandfather's parish. Her father was the leading minister of New Haven, one of the founders of Yale, and the framer of the Saybrook platform. When Edwards was about twenty, and Sarah, seven years younger, he penned a lyrical panegyric of her spiritual loveliness in the vein of a seventeenth-century character.

They say there is a young lady in [New Haven] who is beloved of that Great Being, who made and rules the world, and that there are certain seasons in which this Great Being, in some way or other invisible, comes to her and fills her mind with exceeding sweet delight, and that she hardly cares for anything, except to medi-

[19]

tate on him—that she expects after a while to be received up where he is, to be raised up out of the world and caught up into heaven; being assured that he loves her too well to let her remain at a distance from him always. There she is to dwell with him, and to be ravished with his love and delight forever. Therefore, if you present all the world before her, with the richest of its treasures, she disregards it and cares not for it, and is unmindful of any pain or afflliction. She has a strange sweetness in her mind, and singular purity in her affections; is most just and conscientious in all her conduct; and you could not persuade her to do anything wrong or sinful, if you would give her all the world, lest she should offend this Great Being. She is of a wonderful sweetness, calmness and universal benevolence of mind; especially after this Great Being has manifested himself to her mind. She will sometimes go about from place to place, singing sweetly; and seems to be always full of joy and pleasure; and no one knows for what. She loves to be alone, walking in the fields and groves, and seems to have some one invisible always conversing with her.

Here Edwards reveals the most delicate and endearing qualities of his religion and character: The former appears almost idyllic, and the latter, peaceful and unperturbed. Written in the midst of his studies of Locke and Newton, this sketch shows a philosophical rather than a theological conception of the deity. Significant is his phrase "that Great Being," which he would never have used in a sermon. Indeed one would assume that the sketch had been written by a deist, were it not for the reference to Sarah's being "caught up into heaven." Despite the ethereal, other-worldly impression we are given of her, she adapted easily to earthly business, becoming an efficient housekeeper and gracious hostess and bearing her husband eleven children.

Edwards himself had at least a normal share of amatory temperament. In his private notebooks he actually regretted the limitations of physical love. How soon, he lamented, "do earthly lovers come to an end of their discoveries of each other's beauty! How soon do they see all that is to be seen, are they united as near as 'tis possible and have communion as intimate as possible! How soon do they come to the most endearing expression of love that 'tis possible to come to, so that no new ways can be invented, given, or received." In heaven, Edwards believed, men will experience all the physical pleasures of this world, presumably including sex. "Every part of the saints' refined bodies," he affirmed "shall be as full of pleasure as they can hold, and . . . this will not take the mind off from but prompt and help it in spiritual delights."

In February, 1729, Solomon Stoddard died, and Edwards became sole minister of the Northampton congregation. Although conscientious in his parish duties, as in all else, Edwards delighted more in his studies than in his pastoral rounds. He was always a pulpit minister rather than a family one. His notebooks and catalogues reveal a tremendous amount of reading—but little diversification. Whatever unbeaten tracks he explored, he was always led by some religious quest. He consulted his authorities only to prove or verify predetermined hypotheses, and he showed the Puritan's distrust of purely secular learning. Vain, he warned, are those affections which arise from other than spiritual knowledge.

Indeed this was an underlying theme of Edwards' first published work, *God Glorified in the Work of Redemption, by the Greatness of Man's Dependence upon him, in the Whole of it,* a sermon which he preached on July 8, 1731, in Boston, at the invitation of the ministers of the community. The ancient Greeks had mistakenly sought "human wisdom," he observed in his opening remarks, but it is through Christ alone that true wisdom is imparted to the mind. "The more men exalt themselves, so much the less will they surely be disposed to exalt God." So impressed were the Boston ministers by Edwards' youthful sincerity, strength, and clarity of vision that they published his sermon with a preface complimenting the author, his alma mater Yale College, and his ministerial predecessor Solomon Stoddard. The main theme of the sermon was Edwards' favorite doctrine of grace founded upon the broader doctrine of the absolute dominion of God in the universe. The only novelty of presentation was in a somewhat academic distinction, possibly based on scholastic logic, between the objective good of the redeemed person and his inherent good. His objective good is that object in which he

[21]

finds his happiness—or God. His inherent good is the pleasure of the soul itself as it partakes of the moral image of God. Here is undoubtedly a reflection of the Platonic concept of the effusion of God upon the soul—a concept which Edwards acquired from his profane reading rather than from the Scriptures. Edwards' conclusion, that God is glorified by man's dependence, was almost lost sight of in the steps by which he reached it. He specifically warned against those schemes of divinity which put man in God's stead in any respect: his way of alluding to Arminianism, the *bête noir* of the Calvinists. Edwards was to become the great American leader in the struggle against the new theology—almost the last respectable thinker to be engaged in the cause. His earliest writing foreshadowed the two major principles in his desperate campaign—that nothing but absolute dependence upon God was valid doctrine, and that saving faith had no element of human achievement or merit.

Edwards' next publication, *The Reality of Spiritual Light*, was primarily epistemological, an attempt to show how human response is related to the saving faith dealt with in his previous sermon. Here he considered spiritual wisdom as a part of grace and presented the two together as the highest gift which God can give to man. This spiritual wisdom he delineated as a real sense of the excellency of God, a pleasure and delight in the idea of excellency (the "inherent good" of the previous sermon and the touchstone of genuine conversion as indicated in his "Personal Narrative"). This wisdom is to be distinguished from carnal knowledge just as human conscience is different from the exercise of the spirit of God in the conviction of sin. Reason perceives truth, but the heart alone perceives excellency. By emphasizing an anti-intellectual tradition, Edwards seemed to be encouraging the lowborn and illiterate: perhaps a reason for the popular appeal of his preaching in the first stage of his Northampton pastorship. It was always his principle that his sermons be "clear and plain, accommodated to the capacity of his hearers, and tending to convey light to their understandings."

Shortly before delivering his sermon on spiritual wisdom, Edwards had noticed an improvement in the behavior of the young people of his congregation and began to think in terms of a revival or, as it was expressed in those days, a general "attention to religion." To lead the people to spiritual heights was the ambition of every New England preacher—although the prevailing moral austerity and nearly universal church affiliation made seasons of extraordinary holiness somewhat difficult to produce or to discern after they had come about.

"This is the age of experiments," Benjamin Franklin wrote in his autobiography, and the comment was as true in eighteenth-century religion as in science. Indeed, in the American colonies, Edwards and other exponents of evangelical methods used the expression "experimental religion" to separate their system from conservative Anglicanism and Congregationalism. Edwards believed that each individual should have a personal experience in religious life—that he should feel a dedication to Christ—rather than give mere intellectual assent to a body of doctrine. This emotional response made religion "experimental." In doctrine, the emphasis fell more and more upon the believer's personal feeling and faith—and his justification in heaven by means of this faith—and less and less upon his practical behavior or "works."

Northampton under Solomon Stoddard had known a series of revivals, or "harvests," as he called them, between 1679 and 1718; and during Edwards' boyhood, his father's preaching had wrought the same effect in East Windsor. At the same time that Edwards' own congregation began to show a deeper interest in "experimental religion," the doctrine of Arminianism, which stressed good works and free will, began to make a "great noise" or prevail over large areas of New England, and Edwards decided to combine an exhortation for revival with an onslaught upon the unwelcome doctrine—a decision which brought him at the same time pastoral success and personal controversy. The powerful Williams clan, led by Edwards' own cousin, advised him categorically not to introduce doctrinal polemics into the pulpit and, when he proceeded to do so, opposed him directly and violently.

Undeterred by his critics, Edwards preached in 1734 a stinging, controversial sermon on justification by faith. He later complained that he had been "greatly reproached" for defending the doctrine and that he had suffered "a very open abuse for it." His opponents took over Edwards' anti-intellectual approach to attack the doctrine of justification, condemning it as "too much incumbered with speculative nice-

[23]

ties, and subtle distinctions." Throughout the rest of Edwards' career, this was to be the standard attack upon his theological works—that they were excessively and hopelessly metaphysical rather than practical. Paradoxically, Edwards sought to interpret Scripture for the weakest minds; yet his writings are considered to be about the most abstruse in American theology. In his sermon Edwards defensively declared that "so much of the Scripture scheme of justification as is absolutely necessary to salvation, may be very plain, and level with the understandings of the weakest Christians." Most of the great doctrines of Christianity, he argued, "contain something that is easy, yet they also contain great mysteries," and progress in knowledge of them is possible only through the kind of accurate distinction and close application of thought which he was presenting in his exposition. The Arminian system of justification by our own virtue, he scoffed, may be as plain and natural as can be, but if it is contrary to the Scriptures it must be rejected. Edwards was quite clear about his position: He would follow reason to interpret Scripture, but his final authority was not reason, but Scripture.

Expository sermons such as this one were more likely to arouse the ire of Edwards' Arminian relatives than the emotions of his congregation, but a more forceful hortatory one, "The Justice of God in the Damnation of Sinners," worked upon individual feelings and succeeded in producing what Edwards called a "wonderful pouring out of the spirit of God." In this sermon, moreover, Edwards presented his theological reasons for rejecting the freedom of the will— prefiguring his greatest literary work. He forcefully and directly applied the doctrine of sin to the guilty in his audience who were afraid of damnation—virtually the entire congregation. "How *sensual* have you been?" he asked. "Are there not some here that have debased themselves below the dignity of human nature, by wallowing in sensual filthiness, as swine in the mire, or as filthy vermin feeding with delight on rotten carrion? . . . And what abominable *lasciviousness* have some of you been guilty of! How have you indulged yourself from day to day, and from night to night, in all manner of unclean imaginations! Has not your soul been filled with them, till it has become a hold of foul spirits, and a cage of every unclean and hateful bird?" (Here, as in many other passages, Edwards reveals a Swiftian disgust with human nature seemingly based as much upon physical aversion as upon theological considerations.) After portraying each of his stunned listeners as guilty of slighting God, Edwards wrathfully asked, "Is it a heinous thing for God to slight you, a little, wretched, despicable creature; a worm, a mere nothing, and less than nothing; a vile insect, that has risen up in contempt against the Majesty of heaven and earth." Edwards relentlessly hammered away at his theme: Nobody merits and nobody wills salvation, and no human works are of any value in attaining it. Yet because of God's majesty there "is encouragement for you still to seek and wait, notwithstanding all your wickedness." Passages such as this brought alternating chilly despair and agonizing hope to Edwards' flock. They rushed back to church for assurance, and toward the end of December, 1734, the revival was on. Nearly the whole adult population of the town became communicants; no subject other than religion occupied conversation; and, as Edwards pictured it, despite the fearful motives behind the mass conversions, a religious joy abounded.

The revival reached its height in March and April, 1735, but declined in May as the spring sap rose or, from Edwards' perspective, as Satan intruded. Edwards' uncle, Joseph Hawley, who suffered from melancholia, cut his throat one Sunday morning—and "multitudes" talked of following his example, "as if somebody had spoke to them, *Cut your own throat, now is a good opportunity.*" Edwards preached the funeral sermon on the theme, "We are all in ourselves utterly without any strength or power to help ourselves." His own health suffered—perhaps in part because of the emotional excitement—and he was forced to take a long journey to New York in the fall as a therapeutic measure. Here he met two fiery Calvinists, Gilbert and William Tennent, his theological counterparts from the Philadelphia area, who cheered him with reports of revivals they had been leading in New Jersey.

In the next year, Edwards noted his personal recollections and impressions in *A Faithful Narrative of the Surprising Work of God in the Conversion of Many Hundred Souls in Northampton, and the Neighboring Towns and Villages,* which was published in England in 1737 by the famous hymn

[25]

writer Isaac Watts and another clergyman. These editors heralded the event in Northampton as the first extensive revival recorded in modern times. Up to then the view had been generally held that these upheavals had been confined to apostolic times. Now there seemed to them to be a real possibility of a general movement to bring the kingdom of the Lord upon earth. The English editors also congratulated Edwards upon his preaching "the common plain protestant doctrine of the Reformation, without stretching towards the antinomians on the one side, or the Arminians on the other."

In his narrative Edwards devoted the most space to a detailed and circumstantial account of the conversion of a four-year-old child, Phebe Bartlet, because her story was the most difficult to believe and also because it served to exalt the value of divine wisdom over human.

In March, 1737, occurred the second amazing event in the history of the Northampton congregation—a natural catastrophe which was interpreted in just the reverse manner from that in which the later, world-famous Lisbon earthquake was to be viewed, when Voltaire and hundreds of other thinkers put into question the concept of a benevolent God in the wake of the horrible suffering and death of the innocent inhabitants of Lisbon. Edwards and his congregation had their faith in God strengthened and vindicated by a calamity on a much smaller scale. In the midst of the morning worship, the entire gallery of the Northampton meeting house, filled with people, shrieking and crying, collapsed upon the heads of the others below. "Nothing else was expected than to find many people dead, or dashed to pieces"; but mysteriously and wonderfully every life was preserved. Edwards could only ascribe the marvelous preservation of the exposed multitudes to the benevolence of God and heralded it as "a sufficient argument of a Divine providence over the lives of men." He improved the occasion, nevertheless, by calling a special day of prayer and presenting the accident as a "Rebuke of God and a Loud Call to Repent."

As the revival was proceeding, Edwards' attention was diverted by a matter of ecclesiastical polity. A neighboring council of ministers refused to ordain a minister at Springfield, charging him with immorality and unscriptural doctrine. The churches then called upon a second council, composed largely of Boston ministers, which carried out the ordination. Edwards' uncle, Williams of Hatfield, moderator of the local council, asked Edwards to write a pamphlet defending its action against the Boston ministers, which he proceeded to indite with his usual energy and incisiveness. Like most men of his calling at that time, Edwards had a taste for polemic, and his dedication to defending his favorite doctrines had within it a certain zest for controversy as well as for philosophical truth.

In the section of his "Personal Narrative" devoted to the period of the Northampton revival, Edwards depicted his pleasure in reading of the "advancement of Christ's kingdom upon earth," the light in which he considered the events around him. On one occasion in 1737 when he had ridden into the woods for his health and dismounted from his horse to walk for contemplation and prayer, he reported that the person of Christ appeared to him for about an hour, keeping him in a flood of tears. He felt such an ardor of soul that he wished "to lie in the dust, and to be full of Christ alone." Yet somewhat later, in discussing humility, he rejected the phrase "humbled to the dust" as improper for him, preferring to describe himself as lying "infinitely low before God."

Edwards himself would have been the last to deny that his vision of Christ may have been self-imposed. In a later treatise on religious affections, which some of his contemporaries would have called religious enthusiasm, he devoted a long paragraph to explaining various visions of Christ or the manner by which the imaginations of some men trick them into believing they have had spiritual experiences. "They have had lively ideas of some external shape, and beautiful form of countenance; and this they call spiritually seeing Christ. Some have had impressed upon them ideas of a great outward light; and this they call a spiritual discovery of God's or Christ's glory." Edwards' wealth of detail suggests that he may have experienced a similar delusion.

On a Friday evening in October, 1740, Edwards received a visitor in the person of a fellow clergyman, George Whitefield, eleven years Edwards' junior, who had already made a name for himself in England and who was to become even more famous as the first and greatest of all mass evangelists. Traveling northward from a spectacular campaign in the middle colonies (where he had succeeded in winning the friendship of Benjamin Franklin and creating a climate of opinion which had forced Franklin to curb his deistical propaganda), Whitefield had learned of the triumph of religion in Northampton and had come to compare notes. Bearing the approval of Gilbert and William Tennent, Whitefield adhered to the same standards of doctrinal and moral purity as Edwards. He remained in Northampton less than three full days, during which time he preached five sermons and demonstrated some of the theatrical techniques which had become the marks of his ministry. The two clergymen were equally dedicated to spreading the gospel, but while one was a philosopher, the other was an actor. Edwards was outwardly austere, internally tender and sensitive; Whitefield was outwardly effusive, but inwardly somewhat arid. Although Whitefield was a gifted organizer and could literally bring thousands under his spell during an outdoor sermon, he never enjoyed the matrimonial contentment which blessed the Edwards household. His compulsion to find a wife partly motivated his travels, but he lacked as a suitor the dynamic assurance which he assumed in the pulpit. So impressed was he with Sarah Edwards, "a Daughter of *Abraham*," that he sent up fervent prayers that he might find a similar helpmeet.

Edwards accompanied his guest to the next stop on his itinerary, the house of Edwards' father in East Windsor, and during the course of the journey remonstrated with Whitefield against two of his common tendencies as an evangelist —paying too much attention to emotional impulses and judging other persons to be unconverted. By the first, Whitefield seemed to be making the way of salvation too easy, by the second, too hard. Although Edwards taught the great difficulty of knowing another's heart, it was his practice when he was satisfied concerning the good estate of his own people "to signify it to them." Edwards later felt that his criticism of Whitefield kept the English evangelist from becoming his intimate friend, but they nevertheless always regarded each other with respect and affection. When they parted at East Windsor, Whitefield—always filled with grandiose schemes— confided to Edwards that he planned shortly to bring over to New Jersey from Britain a number of young men to be ordained by the Tennents. In a few months Edwards' knowledge of this scheme was to expose him to another damaging controversy. Whitefield also advocated the employing of laymen to exhort and to teach, and Edwards suggested to Gilbert Tennent that the method be used in America. Tennent turned out to be vigorously opposed, on the grounds that novices and zealots could do great harm—and he, of all people, warned Edwards against the "great hazard of enthusiasm." Edwards himself soon became a vigorous opponent of lay preaching, an attitude derived perhaps from his sense of the importance of the ministerial calling. "If God had not seen it necessary that such things should have certain limits and bounds," he once wrote in a letter reproaching a young man for exhorting a public congregation, "he never would have appointed a certain particular order of men to that work and office."

As part of the revival technique laid down by Whitefield, congregations were to be whipped into ecstasies or agonies by visiting clergymen, who were better equipped to arouse and agitate than the local pastors because their reasoning, rhetoric, and gestures were novelties. When such seasoned evangelists as Whitefield and the Tennents were not in the neighborhood, New England pastors traded pulpits for brief periods. During a large part of the revival in Northampton, Edwards was holding meetings in Leicester, while a certain Rev. Mr. Buell took his place at home. Buell apparently enjoyed as much success as Edwards even with his wife Sarah, whose transports continued with undiminished fervor during the period of her husband's absence.

Gilbert Tennent followed Whitefield to New England at the latter's urging for the express purpose of converting the Bostonians. His pulpit manner was famous for its violence. In general one may say that Edwards reasoned in the pulpit, and Whitefield cajoled, but Tennent raged and threatened as the most direct means of arousing terror in his unconverted hearers. In the summer of 1741, at the village of Enfield, Connecticut, Edwards took a leaf from Tennent's book in his most famous sermon, "Sinners in the Hands of an Angry God." Reverting to his spider image, Edwards pictured God holding the sinner over the pit of hell as "some loathsome insect over the fire . . . ten thousand times more abominable in his eyes, than the most hateful venomous serpent is in ours." In an equally forceful Biblical image, he depicted God in hatred and contempt treading upon the sinner. "He will crush you under his feet without mercy; he will crush out your blood, and make it fly, and it shall be sprinkled on his garments, so as to stain all his raiment." Some of the congregation, he predicted, would be writhing in hell before the next morning! Yet Edwards seemed to offer the same hope as that which any "whosoever will" evangelist held out to induce conversion. "This is a day of mercy," he promised; "you may cry now with some encouragement of obtaining mercy." In private, he may have decided that the regenerate and unregenerate were chosen before the creation of the world, but he certainly concealed the doctrine at Enfield. Because of the general excitement of the revival spirit, Edwards like many of his associates felt that the end of the world was in sight and that God was "hastily gathering in his elect in all parts of the land." As a final appeal to any hesitating sinners at Enfield, therefore, he predicted that "the greater part of adult persons that ever shall be saved, will be brought in now in a little time." Before the sermon was finished, there was moaning throughout the audience, and many cried out —in what had become an almost traditional response—"What shall I do to be saved?" According to an eyewitness, one of Edwards' fellow ministers, "there was such a breathing of distress, and weeping, that the preacher was obliged to speak to the people and desire silence, that he might be heard."

To Edwards, there was nothing particularly harsh or brutal about the Enfield sermon. Throughout his life he believed that "fears of hell tend to convince men of the hardness of their hearts." He employed essentially the same motivation in writing to his own thirteen-year-old daughter, who was visiting in another town. Reminding her that she had "very weak and infirm health" and was likely to die soon and so would not even enjoy many physical comforts for the short time she lived, he concluded that her mortal condition was of little importance. "If your soul prospers," he wrote after his manner of consoling, "you will be a happy, blessed person, whatever becomes of your body."

In 1741, Edwards attended the commencement at New Haven and preached a sermon, *Distinguishing Marks of a Work of the Spirit of God,* a psychological analysis of conversion. Published at the height of the revival ecstasy, or the Great Awakening, it gave Samuel Cooper an opportunity to rejoice in a preface that "the apostolic times seem to have returned upon us" and to appeal to readers to send Edwards accounts of spectacular conversions so that they could be compiled into a narrative, which would perhaps "come the nearest to the Acts of the Apostles of any thing extant." In the audience when Edwards delivered his sermon was an undergraduate, Samuel Hopkins, who had previously been so swayed by the preaching of Gilbert Tennent that he had determined to become a Tennent disciple. But he decided on the spot to adopt Edwards instead as his mentor and resolved to live with him at Northampton, the seat "famous for experimental religion."

By the next year, a reaction had set in against itinerant preaching, mass conversions, and hysterical exhibitionism. The Great Awakening was turning into a nightmare. New England had virtually divided into two camps for and against Whitefield and the new itinerant evangelism. The pro-Whitefield, pro-emotional forces were called New Lights; those who opposed them were called Old Lights, the terms having been used among English Presbyterians before Whitefield ever came to America. Although a partisan of Whitefield, Edwards did not consider himself as a minister of the New Lights but he advocated moderation in dealing with them, particularly urging that members of established congregations who separated to join the New Lights should not be castigated. Much chastened by the new turn of events and no longer viewing the religious fervor as a forerunner of the millennium, Edwards tried to restore a proper perspective and to reduce the strife and uproar by publishing in 1742 *Some Thoughts concerning the Present Revival of Religion*. He argued essentially that there was more good in the recent religious turmoil than bad. Because of his own experience, Edwards made a distinction between sudden revelations or thunderclap conversions and a placid sense of God in the heart, unequivocally preferring "humble joy in God, one quarter of an hour, than . . . prophetical visions and revelations the whole year." Yet by insisting that the events he had analyzed were nevertheless the "glorious work of God," he left no doubt that he was on the side of Whitefield. And although he had recognized that the millennium had not begun, he still regarded the revivals as its forerunners and could not believe that the enemies of the church of God would ever exercise as much power as they had in the past.

A long, circumstantial account of "the highest transports" Edwards had been acquainted with, in a person who had enjoyed heavenly delight for years together, is generally assumed to be a description of the spiritual life of his own wife, Sarah. To be sure, she was the person he knew best, but since her transports "arose from no distemper catched from Mr. *Whitefield,* or Mr. *Tennant,* because they began before either of them came into the country," Edwards was hardly fair in presenting her as a work of "the present revival."

Although Edwards would have nothing to do with the Arminian opinion that good works count toward salvation, he nevertheless insisted that the exercise of charity and good works was the obligation of every Christian. The Christian life, Edwards affirmed, requires the expression of "love to God, by obeying his moral commands of self-denial, righteousness, meekness, and Christian love, in our behaviour among men." In Philadelphia, Franklin read this passage from *Thoughts concerning the . . . Revival* with great approval and cited it to his sister Jane, a staunch Calvinist, in order to support his own view that it is more important to show religion by deeds than by words. Unquestionably, Edwards was vitally concerned with practical ethics as well as with abstract moral excellence, and Franklin is one of the few observers of American religion to have taken the trouble to point this out.

While such evangelists as Whitefield, Tennent, and Edwards were rejoicing in their success in heightening the emotions of the converted and unconverted, a number of traditional clergymen began to protest bitterly against the hysterical outbursts and bodily ecstasies involved in the revival movement. Foremost in the opposition were the faculty of Harvard University and Charles Chauncey, pastor of the influential First Church of Boston. The latter in 1743 published *Seasonable Thoughts on the State of Religion in New England,* an appeal for the restoration of reason as the fundamental element in religion.

In reply to these rationalistic critics, Edwards preached in

1742-43 a series of sermons designed to establish the nature of true religion, or, as he saw it, to vindicate the "experimental" or experiential approach. These sermons he gathered together in 1746 in revised and expanded form as *A Treatise concerning Religious Affections*. As part of his effort to vindicate the role of the affections or emotions in religion, Edwards sought to describe in detail the distinguishing characteristics of those persons who are in favor with God. Although he felt competent to set forth the general criteria, he insisted that no one could ever be sure about his own state of grace—and Edwards' doubts about his own spiritual condition seem to have persisted far beyond this time.

Since time had proved that some of the so-called conversions of the Great Awakening had been merely sham, theatrics, or worse, Edwards admitted that great evils could result from emotional revivals—as he put it, that the devil could mix counterfeit religion with the true. Even in dealing with doctrine, Edwards denounced the evangelical hypocrites—those pharisaical exponents of his own doctrines of justification and free grace who made for themselves a righteousness out of their own humility, like madmen who think they are kings. These zealots Edwards considered to be worse than Arminians.

Although Edwards' treatise on the affections is a pioneering work in psychology—perhaps the most skillful analysis of the emotions written in English up to that time—Edwards insisted upon delineating the revival in doctrinal terms, failing to realize that it was a social phenomenon which temporarily exalted the religious ardor of an extensive geographical area far beyond its normal level.

Because of Edwards' writings and the personal letters of other ministers to their colleagues in Scotland, the religious fervor caught on and raged across the ocean: one of the first instances of the New World influencing the Old. The next, immeasurably greater in impact, would be Franklin's electrical experiments.

In 1744 a group of Scottish ministers, including all of Edwards' correspondents, proposed that they and their congregations engage at stated times during every week in formal prayer for revival and the advancement of Christ's kingdom on earth, which they felt was imminent. Three years later

Edwards published *An Humble Attempt to Promote Explicit Agreement and Visible Union of God's People in Extraordinary Prayer,* supporting the Scottish plan and proposing that the people of America join in the same enterprise. Even after the dismal contretemps of the Northampton revival, Edwards still believed that the "latter times" might be those of his generation. This pamphlet, which now has value only as a curiosity, has the distinction of being the first work by Edwards to be translated into French (in 1823).

In May, 1743, Edwards went to Boston for a convention of the clergy, traveling on horseback with his eldest daughter on a pillion behind him. Upon encountering Thomas Clap, Rector of Yale, with his wife and son-in-law en route to the same meeting, they continued as a group. This pleasant spring journey through the countryside with congenial companions —undoubtedly an agreeable interlude for the hardworking pastor—paradoxically led to another of Edwards' unfortunate personal controversies. During their conversation Edwards revealed Whitefield's plan to bring young men from Britain to be ordained in America, the design of which Clap apparently misunderstood, for he reported publicly the next year at the Harvard commencement that Whitefield "had the design of turning out of their places the greater part of the ministers of New England, and of supplying their pulpits with ministers from England, Scotland, and Ireland." Edwards immediately and forthrightly denied that he had quoted Whitefield to this effect, and he and Clap passed a series of letters backwards and forwards, each justifying himself without directly accusing the other of lying. When each allowed his replies to be published, it was clear that polemics rather than divinity was the motivating force. The fact that these letters could even be published and sold indicates the burning interest in personality which characterized the ordinary citizen of the period. The normal desire for humanizing those in great place was not being satisfied by novels, drama, or the daily newspaper. Unfortunately for Edwards, the controversy virtually closed the gates of Yale to him, although in compensation he was drawn even closer to the College of New Jersey, already congenial because of its ties with the Tennents. The controversy was to Edwards' honor, nevertheless, for beyond demonstrating his loyalty to truth, which no one doubted, he defended Whitefield at the expense of destroying his own good relations with his alma mater.

In his family circle, Edwards may have had a sweet disposition, but to his colleagues and congregation he revealed the same austerity and forbidding exterior which posterity has discovered in much of his writing. It was probably Edwards' difficult personality that inspired another clergyman, named Moody, to compare him unfavorably with his wife, Sarah. One day when Edwards was late for a service where he was to be guest speaker, Moody began the introductory prayer just before Edwards' arrival, which Moody did not notice. During the prayer Moody referred to Edwards' character and ministry in a highly panegyrical vein. Turning around at the end of the prayer and noticing Edwards for the first time, he extended his right hand and remarked, "Brother Edwards, we are all of us much rejoiced to see you here today, and nobody, probably, as much so as myself; but I wish that you might have got in a little sooner, or a little later, or else that I might have heard you when you came in, and known that you were here. I didn't intend to flatter you to your face; but there's one thing I'll tell you: They say that your wife is going to heaven by a shorter road than yourself." One critic has assumed that this was an allusion to "Edwards' lengthened and metaphysical explanations of the doctrines of the church." Certainly Moody was referring to Edwards' tardiness and was probably hitting as well at his deficiencies in human relations.

Edwards' personality was the root of a series of events which led to his separation from the Northampton church, even though other forces—social, political, and theological— were also involved. At the moment when he was writing his treatise on the affections, describing in detail all the qualifications of a Christian saint, most of which he undoubtedly exemplified, the storm was brewing which would lead his congregation to disavow his authority, dissolve the pastoral relation, and cast him and his family of ten children into the wide world. It began in 1744 with a common enough incident—a group of teenagers furtively passing around a naughty book, specifically a manual of midwifery. As the community pastor, Edwards was the logical one to deal with the situation; he preached a sermon on purity, chose a com-

mittee of inquiry, and read out in meeting a list of the young
people who were to be summoned before the committee. It
was bad enough to make any names public; it was worse to
lump together in the list those who were called merely as
witnesses and those who were actually accused of misbehavior. As a result nearly every family in the town, including
the most prominent, had some young member involved—and
the heads of families quickly lost interest in pursuing the
matter. Some of the young people refused to appear before
the committee, others answered with great insolence, and
the whole inquiry was eventually abandoned. The young
people as a group, among whom Edwards had formerly exercised a strong control, lost their respect for religious authority, and his influence as a symbol of pious wisdom declined.
In the midst of the controversy Edwards wrote out self-
questioning notes, indicating awareness of his fallibility:
Should he even have taken notice of the juvenile misbehavior in his role as pastor of the church or would he have
done better to talk with the culprits in private?

The final breach occurred over a question of church polity:
Samuel Stoddard's practice of admitting to the Lord's Supper
those who would partake with the hope of obtaining conversion instead of limiting it to those who were already assured
of their conversion. For at least the first twenty years of his
tenure at Northampton, Edwards had adapted himself to this
compromise, although in his 1734 sermon on "The Justice of
God" he had castigated those who came to the Lord's Supper
with unclean hearts. Eventually he decided that, according
to Scripture, the ordinance was intended only for "*visible*
professing Christians," and in 1748 made public his opposition to Stoddard's way. In his own words, this stand "oc-
casioned great uneasiness among my people, and has filled
all the country with noise." Completely insensitive to social
forces, Edwards doggedly set out to push back the tide of
liberal religion.

Almost before Edwards could make a step he was knocked
off balance by the general cry that he should be dismissed.
He then tried to turn back, but it was too late. The standing
committee of the church rejected his request to be allowed
to preach on the subject, consenting merely to his printing
his opinions, and agreed to hold off a council until his remarks

[36]

were published. Not only did Edwards' career and reputation now hinge on a polemical treatise, but he was under the painful necessity of refuting his beloved grandfather, the only authority who had written on the other side of the question. Since few of his congregation read his treatise when it was published, Edwards went ahead with a series of special sermons on the disputed subject despite the express request of the church committee that he not do so. The outcome could hardly, therefore, be in doubt. Edwards reported to a friend in December, 1749, that most of his congregation "seem to think it greatly concerns 'em to blacken me, & represent me in Odious Colours to the world, to justify their own Conduct— They seem to be sensible that now their Character can't stand unless it be on the ruin of mine." Yet Edwards' own principles kept him from objecting to a decision of his congregation to dismiss him, for he had affirmed in his private notebooks that the right belonged to the people to choose their own pastor, that it is their part "to choose with what food they will be fed, and . . . also . . . to choose with what feeders they will be fed."

The congregation decided to call a council—not to settle the doctrinal question in dispute but to determine whether the pastor and his people could be reconciled. Although Edwards was to choose half of the members of the council, and the church the other half, for weeks both sides debated whether Edwards must be confined to the pro-Stoddard county for his members or whether he should be allowed to go farther afield. These maneuvers clearly indicated that the church had judged and condemned Edwards in advance. By a majority of one vote, the council in June, 1750, decreed an immediate separation between Edwards and his church. Two Sundays later he delivered his farewell sermon, in which he linked his dismissal with the earlier controversy over the misbehavior of the young. "It has been exceedingly grievous to me," he disclosed, "when I have heard of vice, vanity, and disorder among our youth. And so far as I know my heart, that it was from here that I formerly led this church to some measures, for the suppressing vice among our young people, which gave so great offence, and by which I became so obnoxious."

The chief spokesman of the opposition had been Stoddard's

grandson and Edwards' own cousin, Joseph Hawley, a young man of twenty-eight, "of liberal education and notable abilities, . . . a fluent speaker," and, according to Edwards, an open Arminian. Since Hawley was the son of the man who had cut his own throat during the revival turmoil, he may have acted out of revenge or he may have thought it his duty to oppose as fanatical any religious practice associated with Edwards. After Edwards' death, Hawley published an abject confession and contrite apology, assuming guilt for unfair parliamentary maneuvers and for presenting to the council "severe, uncharitable, . . . groundless and slanderous imputations on Mr. Edwards." Publishing the letter was for Joseph akin to his father's slitting his throat. He finally ended his days in insanity.

When Edwards ascended the pulpit for his farewell sermon, he was forty-six years old, unemployed and "thrown upon the wide ocean of the world" with a large and chargeable family. Because of his advanced years, he was not likely to find a similar post in his profession and he was not fitted for any other means of getting a living. Yet the only lesson which Edwards drew from his downfall was that the providence of God continually illustrates "the instability and uncertainty of all things here below."

Although some biographers attribute Edwards' defeat to his alleged aristocratic demeanor and beliefs and suggest that he was seeking to perpetuate the rule of a privileged class by limiting the sacrament, the parallel between piety and social influence is not valid. It is true, as Edwards himself pointed out, that a contention existed between the men of wealth in town and church and an opposing party which was jealous of their power and influence. But the wealthy group comprised mainly Arminians, who stood to suffer by Edwards' exclusion policy. Edwards clearly believed that he as minister should dominate both the wealthy and the common people. The civil and ecclesiastical heads of societies, he felt, should be like the head of the human body, which supplies, animates, and directs, and the people should be like the body, which supports and bears the weight of the head.

Even before the dissension over the sacrament, a continued haggling over Edwards' salary indicated that the requisite bond of mutual love and respect did not exist between pastor and people. There is no more reason to assume that the pastor was inordinately extravagant than that the people of Northampton were inordinately niggardly. Edwards cannot be made into an aristocrat just because his wife appreciated pretty clothes. He may have been retiring and contemplative but was hardly haughty. Also we must not forget that his campaign to institute a covenant has been interpreted in part as an effort to impose an ethical surveillance upon the local businessmen. If any aristocrats can be said to have been involved in the Northampton fracas, they were on the side of the opposition to the pastor.

Edwards himself accused the officers and leading men of the town of imitating Stoddard's "dogmatical temper." Characteristically he traced the sad events in Northampton back to his youth and inexperience during the revivals sixteen years earlier. With more ripeness of judgment, he felt, he would have been able to guide his people in a better manner and "lengthen out the tranquility of the town."

Certainly Edwards was vulnerable for having compromised with a practice which he admitted having considered unscriptural for several years. In one of his sermons before the Northampton crisis he had actually supported Stoddard from the pulpit, preaching that it was the duty of all seekers of salvation—whether true Christians or not—to attend the ordinance of the sacrament. Yet if it is true that his congregation actually hated him—as Perry Miller has concluded—it was probably not because of his inconsistency, or as some have expressed it, his hypocrisy, but because of his difficult personality. After the revivalist glow had worn off, the people of Northampton seized on the best pretext to show their displeasure, and Edwards made their resentment more acute and effectively played into their hands by insisting on his doctrinal punctilio.

There would have been some elements of tragic dignity in Edwards' defeat had he ridden his horse out of Northampton immediately following his last sermon, but he did not at once find another church, nor did Northampton find another pastor. He was asked to fill the pulpit from Sunday to Sunday on a weekly basis, while a committee was considering other candidates, an anticlimax uncomfortable to Edwards and even more so to the congregation. Eventually the people of the

town voted that he no longer be asked to preach in Northampton at all, and for some weeks before his successor was
appointed, "they carried on public worship among themselves, and without any preaching, rather than invite him."
As Edwards put it, "nothing would quiet 'em till they could
see the Town clear of [him] Root & Branch, Name and Rem-
nant."

Superficially these were all pious, honorable people, dedicated to God and to mutual love and charity. Yet they had
torn each other apart over a point of doctrine by no means
fundamental to their religious system. In 1737 Edwards had
published his triumphant *Narrative of the Surprising Work of
God* . . . in Northampton; twelve years later he was writing
sorrowful letters to his ministerial colleagues lamenting the
shocking iniquity and absence of love in the same community.
At one period he was heralding the conversion of nearly the
entire town; at another, subjecting every member of his
congregation to a rigid test of spirituality. Yet there was no
fundamental inconsistency in Edwards' position apart from
his early acceptance of the genuineness of the wholesale
conversions in 1735. Like many others, he had been deceived
by wishful thinking. In his second look at the phenomenon in
Thoughts concerning the Present Revival, he insisted that
more importance be attached to continued piety than to
suddenly induced moments of exhilaration. His position concerning the sacrament represented a similar caution. In
essence, Edwards wanted a thorough rather than a superficial
Christianity. His opponents wanted a more easy-going religion but would not admit it to themselves. Edwards viewed
the people of Northampton as high-spirited, stiff-necked, and
"of a difficult and turbulent temper." One wonders how they
would have described their pastor.

When Joseph Hawley, who, three years later, figured as vil-
lain of the piece, asked his victim's forgiveness in a pathetic
letter of recantation, he engendered little sympathy, because
his change of heart merely gave an additional indication of his
mental confusion and emotional instability. Instead of explaining the motives which led him to become the ringleader of the
anti-Edwards forces, he actually declared that he had agreed
with Edwards that the sacrament should be limited to the pro-
fessedly converted, a detail which he had the good sense to

delete when he later published a public confession. Edwards'
reply shows in contrast a solid intellectual firmness combined
with a stern and inexorable spirit of judgment. It reveals as
much about Edwards' character as any of his writings ever
published, even including his "Personal Narrative." His hurt
was bitter, enduring, and wearying—and his wrath embraced
all the people of Northampton. The community leaders in
an effort to smooth over the dispute had published a statement full of half-regrets, granting among other things that
they had been too censorious on insufficient grounds, but
Edwards refused to concede "that such sort of Reflections
and Retractions as these, will be accepted in the sight of
God as sufficient." In references to him, the Church members
had "seem'd to contrive for the strongest, most severe &
opprobrious aggravating kind of Terms," but in their reflect-
tions on their own conduct they contrived "for the softest,
mildest Terms, to touch their own Faults in the most gentle
manner possible, by the softest Language." Unequivocally
Edwards declared, "the Town & Church lies under great Guilt
in the sight of God." Their contrition had been inadequate,
their humility insufficient. "Palliating & extenuating matters,
and dawbing themselves over with untempered mortar, &
sowing Fig leaves will be in vain before him whose pure
& omniscient Eye is as a Flame of Fire." What had aggravated
their offense, Edwards believed, was that they had injured
him in his office as their spiritual father as well as in his own
person. "Abuse of God's messengers has commonly been the
last sin of an offending backsliding People." Since Hawley
was the ringleader, Edwards affirmed, he might expect to be
distinguished henceforth "by God's Frowns."

Having thus spoken his judgment with "as great a degree
of Impartiality" as he was master of, Edwards signed himself
"your Kinsman & Friend, that sincerely wishes your truest
& greatest wellfare & happiness, in this world & the world to
come."

The tragedy of Edwards' life was not that he vainly dedicated all his efforts to salvaging a religious system that was
doomed to virtual obsolescence. He died with the belief that
his writings would be the instrument for reviving the purity
of faith among his people, and from this point of view he
considered his career a success. Edwards' tragedy was per-

sonal, not intellectual. His religion, which in theory should have brought him inner delight and outward complaisance, failed to inspire his congregation with an enduring affection. The Great Awakening was a fleeting period of excitement, which gave neither Edwards nor his people the blessings it promised. Even Edwards' moments of spiritual rapture never completely overcame his harassing doubts as to whether his conversion was genuine. Trying too hard to reach perfection, Edwards failed to attain the happy life. His greatest pleasures and satisfactions were the small ones derived from his studies and his family. If the dawn and sunset stages of his career, at Yale and Princeton, can be counted successes, the periods of his primary labors and extended endeavors were certainly failures.

While the decision of the people of Northampton still remained uncertain, Edwards had described his plight to his ministerial friends in Scotland. One of the most influential, John Erskine, immediately inquired whether Edwards would be willing to sign the Westminster Confession as a preliminary to accepting a call to some congregation in the Church of Scotland. Edwards replied that he would have no difficulty whatsoever in submitting to the Presbyterian type of church government—particularly after his bitter experience with the Congregational form—but that he hesitated to embark with his family on the long voyage across the Atlantic. This was a fortunate reluctance, since his personality would probably have been even less suited to a Scottish village than to a New England town.

The post which he finally accepted was that of pastor and missionary to the Indians at Stockbridge, Massachusetts, a frontier settlement less than sixty miles westward from Northampton. Even though Edwards did not consider the rigors of pioneer living to be as perilous as crossing the Atlantic, he did not seem to be ideally suited for the task of civilizing Indians. Indeed, because of his academic training, literary activities, and extensive theological knowledge, he was obviously overqualified. Yet other reasons besides his mere need of a job led him to turn westward. As an earnest Christian, he believed that the saving of souls was his paramount duty, and the Indians certainly offered unlimited opportunities for evangelizing. Edwards had already declared in a tract published in 1733 "that this life ought to be so spent by us, as to be only a journey or pilgrimage towards heaven."

Beyond these general motives, which would apply to any Christian, Edwards had a strong personal tie with missionary endeavor through David Brainerd, a saintly worker among the Indians for whom Edwards had developed the attachment of a father and intimate friend. Brainerd had been dismissed from Yale in his sophomore year for a too ardent defense of Whitefield against two faculty members, having remarked that one of them had no more grace than a chair. In 1743, the year when his class was graduating, Brainerd returned to New Haven from his missionary work to petition for a reconciliation and the granting of his degree, but his plea was rejected. Edwards, who witnessed his humble acknowledgment of fault, thereupon became a friend and spiritual advisor.

Suffering from tuberculosis ever since his college days, Brainerd was forced by bad health to leave his Indians in 1747, at which time Edwards invited him to reside under his own roof, where he stayed for a few weeks during the spring, just after his twenty-ninth birthday. Edwards considered his sojourn a blessing for the entire family, and his second daughter, Jerusha, then seventeen, fell deeply in love with the young man. Following his physician's advice, Brainerd journeyed to Boston under the care of Jerusha, but in a short time returned to Northampton, where he gradually declined. On the Sunday before his death, he smiled at his fiancée and said, "Dear Jerusha, are you willing to part with me? —I am quite willing to part with you: I am willing to part with my dear brother John, although I love him the best of any creature living. . . . though if I thought I should not see you and be happy with you in another world, I could not bear to part with you. But we shall spend a happy eternity together." Jerusha herself died just four months after Brainerd, and Edwards found consolation in the conviction that they would meet in heaven.

For the entire Edwards family Brainerd was the exemplar of a saint and a Christian hero. Indeed Edwards considered it a distinguishing sign of divine providence that Brainerd was sent to pass his last days in their house. In the midst of the controversy with his congregation, Edwards as a labor of love wrote a long and painstaking *Account of the Life of the Late Reverend Mr. David Brainerd,* which he published in 1749. Since Edwards admitted that this occupation diverted him from his great mission of "publishing something against some of the Arminian tenets," the project which culminated in his treatise on the will, it is obvious that he considered his biography of almost equal importance. In literary history, it made its mark as the first American biography to be translated into another tongue, Dutch, and to achieve wide British circulation. Holland was the other country besides Scotland where the influence of the New England revivals spread and generated new enthusiasm.

In his biographical study, Edwards made the particular points that Brainerd's religion was not limited to emotional experience but was reflected in daily life, and that his example should excite to rigorous attention to duty those who are called to the work of the ministry. Brainerd had genuine compassion for the Indians, which feeling he undoubtedly communicated to Edwards in their fervent conversations. Edwards subscribed to the notion that the Indians had literally been brought to the American continent by the Devil: that Satan, alarmed by the success of the Gospel during the first three centuries after Christ and afraid that his own power might be entirely overthrown in the world, had led a group of people from the East to the West so that they might increase and build him a new kingdom where he could reign as God. Although Brainerd spoke, as was the custom among members of missionary societies, of "these poor heathen" under the bondage of the powers of darkness, he also referred to "the poor Indians" and to his "dear christian Indians." Most important to Edwards' decision was the fact that Stockbridge, which would be the seat of his missionary activities, had been the administrative center at the time of Brainerd's earliest labor with the Indians.

Edwards' negotiations with Stockbridge began after Ezra Stiles, future president of Yale, turned down the missionary post in September, 1750. Edwards' candidacy was sponsored by his disciple Samuel Hopkins, who had also been one of Brainerd's friends. After receiving a formal invitation from the Commissioners for Indian Affairs in December, Edwards preached to both whites and Indians in Stockbridge during the next three months and finally accepted the call after receiving the advice of a council of Northampton citizens which met in May, 1751.

The original plans to establish a missionary settlement at Stockbridge had been set in motion in Northampton, through the initiative and energy of one of Edwards' parishioners, Col. John Stoddard, an expert in Indian affairs, who recommended the site because the Indians there were not under French influence. Several members of the Williams family had promoted the establishment of the mission and school, and Ephraim Williams, whose daughter married the first missionary, purchased land and settled at Stockbridge with the encouragement of the commissioners. The plan was to demonstrate to the Indians the advantages of civilized society by showing them a few selected white settlers as examples and to provide formal instruction for the young. Edwards was expected to be pastor and supervisor of the schoolmaster for the Indians, as well as pastor for the white colony, thus being obliged to hold two sets of services. His salary came from multiple sources—partly from the London Society for the Propagation of the Gospel through the Boston Commissioners for Indian Affairs, partly from the legislature of the colony, and partly from the parish at Stockbridge. Funds for a separate Indian school were provided by an English philanthropist, Isaac Hollis, who made an annual donation conditioned upon the maintaining of twelve Indian boys in the school.

Edwards' freedom as an administrator was severely limited by these complicated arrangements. To make matters worse, the Williams family had a vested interest in every branch of the mission. Edwards, we will remember, had alienated part of the Williams clan by preaching against Arminianism in 1734; Solomon Williams showed that the animosity still existed in 1751 by penning the rebuttal to Edwards' position on sacramental qualifications. At the very moment when Edwards moved with his family to Stockbridge, he was working on an answer to Solomon. Elisha Williams, Edwards' cousin and former tutor at Yale, was soon elevated to become a member of the governing board of the mission; and eventually the man appointed by the commissioners as resident agent married Ephraim Williams' daughter, widow of the original missionary. Edwards was thus effectively delivered into the rough hands of his antagonistic relatives. Although not open enemies, they had no strong desire to cooperate with the pastor, and their secular interests occasionally turned out to be contrary to those of Edwards' Indian charges. Ephraim Williams, Jr., who characterized Edwards as a "very great bigot," represented the attitude of the family. He was willing to have Edwards in Stockbridge, however, since his coming would raise the price of Williams' land.

In June, 1751, Edwards began his work at the settlement, although the ceremony of installation did not take place until August. Here his major problems were not theological but pedagogical, and political to a great extent—and his acute mind immediately produced practical and original solutions.

By applying his philosophical notions to local instructional problems, he conceived a theory of education more advanced than any that would be produced by his countrymen for over a century. In a letter to Isaac Hollis early in July Edwards briefly described the Indian schools at Stockbridge: one for the local Housatonics, sponsored by the Boston commissioners, and the other, sponsored by Hollis, attended by Mohawks brought in from outlying districts. In his letter Edwards declared that the instruction heretofore had been virtually useless, since the Indians were not being taught English as a preliminary step. They obviously could make little headway in learning the art of reading if they did not know the language to start with. In Edwards' words: "They merely learn to make such and such sounds, on the sight of such and such marks, but know not *the meaning* of the words, and so have neither profit nor pleasure in reading, and will therefore be apt soon to lose even what they have learned, having no benefit or entertainment in the use of it." The Indians must henceforth be taught English—and Edwards hit upon a simple, quick, and economical means of doing it: integration. Either the white children must be introduced into the Indian school as classmates of the natives, or else the settlement families must accept Indian children into their homes to reside for a year or two until they should acquire English.

Edwards extended his criticism of the teaching methods for Indians to embrace the entire educational system in the British world. To him, one of the gross defects of "the ordinary method of teaching among the English" was its emphasis on learning without understanding. The children were taught to read a text, that is, to pronounce the words which made it up, without knowing what it meant. They were taught their catechism in like manner: repeating by rote without comprehending the words they uttered. Edwards proposed, therefore, that "the children should never read a lesson, without the master or mistress taking care, that the child be made to attend to, and understand, the meaning of the words and sentences which it reads; at least after the child begins to read without spelling, and perhaps in some degree before. And the child should be taught to understand *things*, as well as *words*." The last sentence indicates that Edwards' pedagogical theories rested on a solid philosophical foundation. That Edwards came to this position through his reading of Locke, who first taught the world the relationship between words and ideas, can be demonstrated by comparing the systems for teaching the deaf in vogue in France and in England during the eighteenth century. French teachers, who freely acknowledge their indebtedness to Locke, developed a sign language to teach the deaf ideas—even though this language had no resemblance to conventional speech. But the English, completely ignoring the notions of Locke, struggled along with the ancient and completely unsuccessful method of requiring the deaf to produce conventional words by imitating lip and larynx movements. Edwards, as a pedagogue, was closer in his methods to French Roman Catholic priests than to any of his own countrymen.

To teach ideas as well as words, Edwards maintained, would accustom the child from infancy to think and reflect and "beget in it an early taste for knowledge." More important, from his point of view, printed catechisms should be supplemented by explanations of the concepts involved, and, if possible, "the child should be led, by wise and skilful management, into the habit of conversation on divine things, and should gradually be divested of that shyness and backwardness, usually discovered in children, to converse on such topics with their superiors." Edwards had not forgotten Phebe Bartlet.

Edwards used a visual method in the teaching of mathematics. He once convinced a thirteen-year-old boy that a two-inch cube is eight times as large as a cube one inch square by cutting out two cubes of these measurements and then cutting the two-inch cube into eight equal parts. The boy counted the parts over and over, compared them one by one with the one-inch cube, and "seemed to be astonished, as though there were some witchcraft in the case."

In reference to his Indians, Edwards advocated that both girls and boys be taught spelling, writing, and arithmetic. And, to promote the great end in view of "leading them to renounce the coarseness, and filth, and degradation, of savage life" (Edwards knew from first-hand experience what a real Indian was like!), he suggested that they be taught singing. "Music," he believed, "especially sacred music, has a powerful efficacy to soften the heart into tenderness, to harmonize the affections, and to give the mind a relish for objects of a superior character."

Edwards' role as a political theorist grew out of a trip in June, 1751, to Albany, where he had gone at the request of the Boston commissioners to observe the making of an Indian treaty. While there he learned of the efforts of the French to gain the friendship of the six Mohawk nations and came to understand the importance of the English making counter-efforts to retain their good will. An Indian expert, Col. William Johnson, told him that "unless something extraordinary was speedily done, and what was never like to be done, these Nations were lost to the British Interest." And an "eminent Mohawk" revealed to Edwards that most of his nation had already been won over to the French: "They indeed come to Albany and treat with the English as Friends; but then go directly to the Governor of Canada, and tell him all that has passed: They speak . . . smooth Words, pleasant Words to the English, but their Hearts are with the French." Edwards also learned one reason why the Indians favored the French: "They could not live with the English, they gave them so much Rum, which they found by Experience wasted them exceedingly."

Shortly after Edwards' formal installation at Stockbridge in August, the commissioners opened a two-week conference with the Mohawk chiefs, negotiating an agreement for these tribes to send their children to the Stockbridge school. On the last day of the month Edwards wrote a lengthy analysis of the situation to Thomas Hubbard, Speaker of the House of the Massachusetts Assembly. Underscoring the dangers from the French, he affirmed the necessity of improving relations with all the Indian tribes, particularly those which were willing to cooperate with the Stockbridge project. After expounding his theories of education, he suggested the appointment of a teacher who would learn the Mohawk language as well as a resident trustee or agent, who would directly represent the interests of the commissioners and handle all the accounts. The latter arrangement should have guaranteed him greater independence from the Williamses, but unfortunately the agent who was eventually appointed—Joseph Dwight —frustrated this intention by marrying Ephraim Williams' widowed daughter.

Excerpts from Edwards' letter were printed by Benjamin Franklin in his *Pennsylvania Gazette* (Oct. 31). It may be that Edwards sent a copy to Gilbert Tennent and that Tennent then turned it over for publication to Franklin, who was something of an expert on Indian affairs in his own right. With the skill of a career diplomat, Edwards portrayed the operation at Stockbridge as essential to the national interest. "The only remaining Means that Divine Providence has left in our Power to regain and secure the Indians in the English Interest, is this very Thing, viz. To our utmost to prosecute the Design of thoroughly *instructing them in the true Protestant Religion, and educating their Children in useful Knowledge.* Colonel Johnson owns this; and says, he knows it will be for the British Interest, for them to prosecute what they have begun at Stockbridge. And now the Most High seems to be opening the Door in an unusual Manner; the Opportunity may be easily lost through our Negligence; for some of the Mohawks themselves are watching for an Opportunity to possess the Minds of those Indians that are inclin'd to Religion, with an Opinion of the Treachery of the English, and to insult those that seem now disposed to trust us, on our disappointing them."

Edwards' somewhat romantic conception of the national importance of his mission dimmed as he began catechizing the Indian boys, listening to their complaints, and delivering watered-down sermons. In theory his pedagogical methods were in advance of his age, but in practice he used the standard device of requiring a student to copy over and over a pious reflection or useful precept. One of the writing exercises that has survived, a scrap of paper on which an Indian had painfully copied, "He that pities another thinks on himself," represents a rather odd sentiment for Edwards, resembling more the cynicism of La Rochefoucauld than the rigorous morality of Puritanism.

Edwards' preaching to the Indians contained much more in the way of exhortation to Christian living—particularly in avoiding the vice of drunkenness—than exposition of Calvinistic doctrine. Sometimes, however, he ingeniously adapted to the uncomplicated minds of his Indians points of doctrine which he had previously expounded in Northampton. Once, for example, he had grimly reminded the people of Northampton that "it is a doctrine which has ever been taught you, and used for the warning, awakening, and humbling of gospel sinners, that they have greater guilt, and are exposed to a more terrible punishment, than the *heathen*." Adapting this concept to his primitive audience, he explained, "You have greater Light than other Indians, but if you go on in sin your Light will do you no good but Hurt. . . . You know your Duty more than others, & G. has done more for you than others & therefore if you dont do your duty you will have a hotter Place in Hell than the Heathen that never heard of J. X."

Despite the difficulties which Edwards faced in providing for his family and the incessant wrangling which the Williamses forced upon him, there was not the slightest trace of self-pity in any of his private letters. Although the first months at Stockbridge were financially stringent, Edwards wrote to his father that he and his wife were pleased with their situation and that the Indians were pleased with his whole family, particularly with his wife. Before Edwards was able to sell his house at Northampton he was forced to buy another at Stockbridge, and during the difficult interim period his daughters helped him carry a debt of two thousand pounds by making lace, painting fans, and embroidering materials for sale in Boston. Edwards himself was sometimes reduced to writing on scraps left over from the fans in order to economize on paper.

In February, 1752, Edwards was delighted by the arrival of a new schoolmaster, Gideon Hawley, a young man inspired by Edwards' *Life of Brainerd* to emulate the saintly missionary. Naturally he became Edwards' "most faithful and useful coadjutor."

Then, all of a sudden, Ephraim Williams' hostility flared out openly in the wake of a new development in London. Joseph Paine and the other trustees of the London Society for the Propagation of the Gospel were advocating the opening at Stockbridge of a girls' boarding school, and Elisha Williams, who was on the spot, was promoting Abigail Williams, married to the agent Joseph Dwight, for the job of headmistress. When the board of commissioners in Boston asked Edwards' opinion as to whether the appointment should be confirmed, he spoke out unequivocally against it. Edwards saw many things wrong with the way money was being poured into Stockbridge—most of it going through the hands of the Williamses, if not into their pockets—but the worst abuse, he felt, was the proposal to appoint Mrs. Dwight. She would be in sole charge of the school, her nearest relatives would be her supervisors, and her husband the only auditor of her accounts.

Edwards had not originally intended to interfere in any way with the female school, but when his advice was particularly asked, he felt that God had commanded him to speak. "If I should hold my peace now, I should perhaps lay a foundation for great uneasiness to my conscience all my life after."

Late in April, 1752, a friend of the schoolmaster whom Hawley had replaced, visited the boys' school and without provocation struck the son of an Onohquauga chief on the head with his cane. When the outraged mother roused the other Indians to the point of taking their children out of the school, Hawley and his interpreter ran to Edwards for advice. Edwards referred them to Dwight, on the grounds that he would no longer subject himself to the accusation of intervening in affairs which did not concern him. Dwight, however, charged him with keeping his hands off only because the affair would be embarrassing to Dwight, a suspicion which probably had some foundation. In the meantime, the Indian chiefs went in a body to Edwards for redress and, finding the aggressor in his company, persuaded the latter to pay damages. This further infuriated Dwight, who stalked into the boarding school and berated Hawley in front of his pupils in a loud voice for three hours. The Indians thereupon threatened to leave the school if any harm should befall Hawley or if he were not retained in his post.

Edwards reported this fracas to the commissioners together with a detailed account of the devices by which Dwight intended to put money into his own pocket: taking over the boys provided for by Hollis, provisioning both schools from his own stores, and introducing his son as master of the boarding school. Beyond this, his wife was to be mistress of the female school, four of their children were to be educated at public expense, one of his family was to be assistant mistress, his servants were to be paid for out of school funds, the house for the boarding school was to be located on his wife's land and later sold at a high rate, and he was to carry on a monopoly trade with the Indians. "A man," Edwards concluded with great reserve, "had need to have a great stock of assuredness, to urge a public affair, under so manifold temptations of private interest." The Williamses retaliated by circulating reports that Edwards was to be removed from the mission, and they made an unsuccessful attempt to carry the point.

By the middle of the summer Edwards finished his final pronouncement on the sacrament controversy, which he published under a title not likely to endear himself to his opponent—*Misrepresentation Corrected, and Truth Vindicated, in a Reply to the Rev. Mr. Solomon Williams's Book.* Writing in the polemical style of the time, Edwards took every pain to make his opponent look ridiculous by emphasizing his faults, questioning his authority, and impeaching his logic. At the same time Edwards "delivered his soul" and obtained what in another man would have been called revenge. In an appendix he addressed his former congregation at Northampton, warning them that the principles which Williams had adopted to defend Stoddard's position on the sacrament were those which Stoddard himself would have considered pernicious and of fatal tendency to the souls of men, and that they contradicted the good and sound doctrines of Williams's previous books. These bad principles, which, according to Edwards, had been introduced into New England through the corrupting influence of John Taylor of Norwich, represented "the new, fashionable, lax schemes of divinity," schemes which undermined the sound doctrines

[52]

which Edwards had formally taught his flock: "eternal election, conversion, justification; and so, of a natural state of death in sin; and the whole doctrine of original sin, and of the mighty change made in the soul by the redemption of Christ applied to it." The *Reply* strongly suggests that Edwards dreaded the melancholy prospect of the spread of Arminianism largely because it was new, contrary to the old and familiar, and would "doubtless by degrees put an end to what used to be called saving religion," the system on which Edwards had based his intellectual life.

In replying to Williams, Edwards adopted a familiar argument in Christian apologetics—that one must not judge the single parts of a theological system, but the entire system; in other words, that a particular doctrine should not be rejected as contrary to reason if the system as a whole is rational, and a particular doctrine, harmless in itself, should not be accepted if the system as a whole is pernicious.

One cannot help feeling that in the actual management of his mission Edwards reversed this emphasis and allowed himself to be overwhelmed by details. There is something anomalous in the philosopher of the will becoming embroiled in a controversy over nepotism in a boarding school for Indian girls. Even though the Williamses were guilty of everything Edwards charged them with, at the most this meant that they took advantage of their position to gain some personal profit. Also, all the documents which have survived reflect Edwards' point of view. In theology and in practical life, Edwards lacked the spirit of accommodation. Certainly he would have been happier at Stockbridge—and the mission would have been more successful—if he had gone about his own work and left the Williamses to themselves or, better still, if he had cooperated with them.

The showdown and Edwards' final victory over the Williamses came on the heels of a last desperate effort by Ephraim to gain control at Stockbridge. One morning in the fall of 1752, Ephraim arose before daybreak and routed out his neighbors from their beds, offering to buy their farms at high cash prices. By noon he had made the rounds of most of the inhabitants, but more thought him crazy than accepted his offer. As a result of this failure, Ephraim gave up his own property and moved away from the settlement. At about this

time Edwards in his writings introduced a new note in referring to his troubles at Stockbridge, now considering them as
a legacy from Northampton. The Williamses he described as
"a family of some note, who vigorously abetted and set for-
ward my opposers at Northampton, and were a chief occasion of my removal from that town." In other words, he
recognized that the contention was more a matter of per-
sonalities than a conflict of interests. After Ephraim moved
away, the chief thorn in Edwards' flesh became the Indian
agent Joseph Dwight, who had been one of his friends and
loyal supporters in Northampton but had moved into the
Williams camp after marrying Ephraim's daughter. Dwight
was naturally displeased by Edwards' attempts to block his
wife's candidacy for the post of schoolmistress and he retaliated by leveling various charges against Edwards in his
annual report to the legislature. He accused Edwards of introducing an unnecessary master in the school, of advancing
the interpreter to the post of assistant instructor, and of opposing Mrs. Dwight. More seriously, he alleged that the
school had declined after Edwards' protégé Hawley had
taken charge, and that Edwards himself was unqualified for
his post because his advanced age had kept him from learning the Indian language. Edwards had little trouble refuting
these charges in a letter to the speaker of the Assembly
offering sufficient evidence that the Indians were pleased with
Hawley and citing the testimony of the preceding missionary
that it would be a waste of time for his successor to attempt
to learn the native tongue. The commissioners supported
Edwards—and the battle was won. Even when the conflict
had been at its height, Edwards could report that he lived
"in peace and friendship, with the generality of the people."

In the midst of his private difficulties at Stockbridge, Edwards did not allow his attention to wander from the spiritual
conflict in the external world between conventional and
modern theology. For him, the struggle was to the death, and
he felt that the other side was no less dedicated, observing
that "these modern fashionable opinions, however called
noble and liberal, are commonly attended, not only with a
haughty contempt, but an inward malignant bitterness of
heart, towards all the zealous professors and defenders of the
contrary spiritual principles, that do so nearly concern the

vitals of religion, and the power of experimental religion."

Therefore, after publishing his reply to Solomon Williams, Edwards prepared to resume his project of writing more directly against Arminianism. A time of crisis, he felt, was imminent, "things . . . going down hill so fast, and truth and religion, both of heart and practice, . . . departing by such swift steps." He confided to John Erskine in the summer of 1752 that the great subject he had chosen was that of free will and moral agency, and that he proposed "to consider the nature of that freedom of moral agents, which makes them the proper subjects of moral government, moral precepts, councils, calls, motives, persuasions, promises and threatenings, praise and blame, rewards and punishments: strictly examining the modern notions of these things, endeavouring to demonstrate their most palpable inconsistency and absurdity; endeavouring also to bring the late great objections and outcries against Calvinistic divinity, from these topics, to the test of the strictest reasoning; and particularly that great objection, in which the modern writers have so much gloried . . . that the Calvinistic notions of God's moral government are contrary to the common sense of mankind."

The following spring, news came that his fourteen-year-old son Timothy had been stricken with a violent fever in New York. Not knowing whether it was the invariably fatal smallpox or a mild form of fever, Edwards immediately wrote to urge him to seek his salvation as the only matter of consequence. If Timothy should die, Edwards wrote, he should feel comforted that he had already taken a final and everlasting leave of his friends, and if he should survive, it would be due to a remarkable providence. "Whatever your circumstances are," he wrote, "it is your duty not to despair, but to hope in infinite mercy, through a Redeemer. For God makes it your duty to pray to him for mercy; which would not be your duty, if it was allowable for you to despair." There is an astounding parallel to this manner of reasoning to be found in Franklin's letters—but Franklin used the evidence of prayer as an argument against necessity. "I reasoned," wrote Franklin, "that if all things are ordained, prayer must among the rest be ordained. But as prayer can produce no change in things that are ordained, praying must be useless and an absurdity. God would therefore not ordain praying if everything else was ordained. But praying exists, therefore all things are not ordained." Reasoning from exactly the same premise—that God requires human beings to pray—Edwards and Franklin upheld completely opposite systems.

After 1754, Edwards' post at Stockbridge developed into a comparative sinecure, the number of Indians present at the inception of his work (two hundred and fifty) having steadily dwindled. The entire Mohawk contingent decamped, and the remaining Housatonics or "Stockbridge Indians" were caught up in the political manipulations of the French and British. Now freed from the harassment of the Williamses, Edwards had few regular responsibilities beyond ministering to his small English congregation and was able to give almost full attention to his theological investigations.

He had resumed writing his treatise on the will in late November, 1752, apparently having previously covered only a few preliminary matters, even though the project had been on his mind for some time. He completed the first draft by the middle of April of the following year, that is, in a period of four and a half months—an extraordinary achievement. His declared purpose, as we have seen, was to refute such English opponents of Calvin as Whitby and Taylor, who argued that acts which are predetermined are devoid of ethical significance—that they cannot be adjudged either moral or immoral. They protested that salvation in the Christian sense requires the assent and adherence of an individual who is completely free to make a choice. Edwards set out to reconcile the Calvinistic doctrine that man's will is irrevocably fixed with the general view of man as a moral agent.

There are two divergent opinions concerning the treatise: one maintains that it raises Edwards as a metaphysician to the same rank as Locke and Leibniz; the other, that it is a "tedious discussion, . . . a solemn bit of special pleading, rather than a disinterested effort to reach the truth." Most people at the present time are likely to agree with the second view, and even in the eighteenth century few besides Scottish and American Puritans accepted the first. The work was adopted by Yale as a textbook in 1762, but after thirteen years was dropped for "giving offense." Most theologians felt that the concept of absolute necessity had too much in common with the materialistic systems of Hobbes, Anthony Collins, and other "infidel" philosophers.

But there is no doubt that Edwards' work is the most thorough and encyclopedic treatment of its subject ever printed. Virtually every relevant argument or ramification of an argument is here presented. Yet Edwards was by no means the last to write on the subject; neither did he exhaust it, as many people believe, nor was his position untenable. Many other necessitarians came after him in that century—some even more famous, such as Joseph Priestley and William Godwin.

The keystone of Edwards' treatise is a paradox previously associated with Hobbes: Freedom from coercion may exist along with necessity to carry out a certain action. The will at any given moment is at liberty to make any of a multitude of different choices, but it is determined by preceding causes to make only a certain one. We have, for example, complete liberty to stand up or to remain seated, but our choosing to do one or the other is based on antecedent causes over which we have no control.

Between July and December, 1754, Edwards was almost totally incapacitated by a fever, the "longest and most tedious" sickness of his life, which reduced him almost to a skeleton. Fits of ague sometimes shook him so severely that he could not hold his pen to write. This sickness together with the death of a friend in the ministry in Scotland put him in a frame of mind to prepare for his own imminent death.

But he recovered the following spring and he began composing the two treatises which, according to many critics, contain his most original philosophical thought: "A Dissertation concerning the Nature of True Virtue" and "A Dissertation concerning the End for which God created the World." Left in manuscript at his death, they were first published in 1788. Together with another posthumously published work, an essay on the Trinity, these treatises represent Edwards' best formal attempt at pure philosophy—reasoning independent of scriptural or dogmatic authority. Although he never freed himself completely from his doctrinal bias, he showed in his approach to the problems dealt with in these works that he was trying to satisfy himself of the truth of things, not merely to batter down an opponent or convince a sluggish congregation. Relatively little attention had been given to creation itself in the teleology of Edwards' day, but the nature of virtue was probably the most discussed subject of the eighteenth century, occupying the attention of practically the entire world of letters—novelists such as Fielding, poets such as Pope, philosophers such as Shaftesbury, and theologians such as Bishop Butler. Edwards' answer, that happiness is the end of virtue, is in itself nothing new, being merely a restatement of ancient Greek ethos, Edwards, however, associated the happiness of the individual with the happiness of God in a novel fashion, making his two treatises companion pieces. Although both demonstrate his obvious acquaintance with the theories of the major moralists of the century, his thought clearly develops the principles foreshadowed in his youthful notes on "Mind."

Despite the silencing of Edwards' personal enemies, obstacles in the way of his missionary activity came from another quarter in 1754 and 1755. This was the period when the French were consolidating their Indian allies and making plans for a general attack on the British western outposts. While Franklin was attempting to persuade Pennsylvania that the colonies must join together or die, and when the best political minds of the colonies were meeting at the Albany Congress, Stockbridge was being turned into a garrison. The Stockbridge Indians, already uneasy because of the general preparations for war, began to feel increased resentment toward the English. Two white travelers had killed an Indian in the woods and had been let off with a very light sentence. This action alienated the entire local Indian population. One Sunday between services some Canadian Indians entered the settlement and killed four whites. When a reward was offered for a Canadian scalp, two foolish white residents dug up the body of a local Indian and tried to palm off his scalp for the reward. Although these rascals were punished for their stupidity, the disgusted Indians became ever more refractory. Edwards' narrative of these events and his analysis of their broader significance show almost the same realism and political discernment which may be found in Franklin's letters of the same period. In December, 1755, after Braddock's disastrous defeat, Edwards reported to Erskine that despite the vast expenditure of money and human blood, the British situation was worse than it had been at the beginning of the year. "It is apparent," he wrote, "that the ministry at home miss it very much, in sending over British forces to fight with Indians in America, and in sending over British officers, to have the command of our American forces. Let them send us arms, ammunition, money, and shipping; and let New England men manage the business in their own way, who alone understand it." No political writer for the colonial press better stated the case.

To another correspondent Edwards gave an acute analysis of the reason for the French military success. "They vastly exceed us in subtilty and intrigue, in vigilance and activity, in speed and secrecy; in acquaintance with the continent of North America," and in skillful handling of the Indians. Moreover, during the war they had the vast advantage of a single absolute commander, the Governor of Canada, "while we are divided into a great many distinct governments, independent one of another, and, in some respects, of clashing interests."

Because of the general fear in late spring, 1756, that a British expedition against Crown Point would be defeated, Edwards' young disciple Joseph Bellamy became alarmed for Edwards' safety and invited him and his whole family to take refuge at Bethlehem. But Edwards remained fast at Stockbridge, spending most of his leisure hours writing a new treatise on original sin. He directed his fire toward the objections to the doctrine found in the works of John Taylor, whom Edwards bluntly described as a "specious writer." Since the treatise on the will was specifically designed for other theologians, Edwards had made no attempt to adapt his abstruse passages to the abilities of the ordinary reader. His first editor maintained, however, that the work on original sin was carefully fitted to a general audience of "lower capacities," but this care seems to have been exercised chiefly in the translation of Latin quotations into English. Otherwise it is every bit as "metaphysical" as the preceding treatise and even more loaded with controversy against latitudinarian writers. The title page, in addition to a verse from Scripture in English, included two Latin epigraphs and a verse from Juvenal: the first time an Edwards' pamphlet had appeared with support from secular letters. The verse from Juvenal, repeated in the text along with parallel citations from Plato, Seneca, and Plutarch, certainly makes man appear as corrupt as Edwards could have wished.

Soon after Edwards' treatise on the will began to circulate in Scotland, a number of the admirers of an eccentric Scottish metaphysician and jurist, Henry Homes, Lord Kames, affirmed that Edwards' position on necessitarianism was essentially the same as that which Kames had expounded in a volume of vaguely deistical essays, *On the Principles of Morality and Natural Religion* (1751). Kames's followers eagerly seized upon the orthodox prestige of the New England divine to exalt their friend's metaphysical profundity. Edwards read Kames's essay in 1755, along with a book of David Hume, later remarking to Erskine, "I am glad of an opportunity to read such corrupt books, especially when written by men of considerable genius; that I may have an idea of the notions that prevail in our nation." When he later heard that Kames's ideas were being compared to his own, Edwards pointed out in detail that the two systems were completely discordant, and that Kames's principles were inconsistent even with each other. The distinction which Edwards made between his system and the Scottish lawyer's hinges chiefly on Edwards' definition of liberty—as indeed does Edwards' entire treatise on the will. Edwards maintained against Kames that liberty of choice may coexist with predetermination of action and that moral relations should be more properly called certain than necessary. Edwards scoffed at Kames's theory that all men's minds are implanted with an illusory notion of liberty —and he argued earnestly, in contrast to the Scottish jurist, that men must be held accountable for their moral behavior. Anticipating the objection which was soon to be raised in force against his own system, Edwards concluded by affirming that no danger lay in the contemplation and discovery of such ideas and that philosophical truth need not be concealed.

A month later in another letter to Erskine, Edwards took note of the opinion of some people, "that if it be really true, that there is no self-determining power in the will as opposed to any such moral necessity, as I speak of, consisting in a certain connexion between motives and volitions, it is of a mischievous tendency to say anything of it; and that it is best that the truth in this matter should not be known by any means." Instead of answering the objection, however, Edwards limited himself to pointing out the pernicious results of the contrary system: "the notion of liberty, consisting in a *contingent self-determination of the will,* as necessary to the morality of men's dispositions and actions." Systems of religion based on this premise, he charged, were "a kind of infidel scheme." They encourage sinners to depend on their own righteousness: "They justify themselves in the sincerity of their endeavours. They say to themselves, that they do what they can; they take great pains; and though there be great imperfection in what they do, and many evils of the heart arise, yet these they cannot help." The notion of a self-determining will teaches moreover that our merit derives from ourselves "as its determining cause, and its original and highest source"; it also keeps man from praying for grace. Edwards insisted that all the glory of salvation should be given to God—the contrary system gives it to man.

As he considers self-reliance in religion and morality as the height of the pernicious, Edwards is worlds away from Emerson, to whom he is often—and ineptly—compared. For Edwards and all the conservative theologians of his milieu, God was all, and man, nothing. Man had no freedom of will and could not even cry out for salvation unless his plea were initiated by God's grace.

On September 24, 1757, Edwards' son-in-law Aaron Burr, president of the College of New Jersey, died unexpectedly of a fever aggravated by a hasty trip from Philadelphia to Elizabethtown to preach the funeral sermon of Governor Belcher. Two days later the corporation of the College nominated Edwards as its choice for the next president.

The invitation came as a surprise to Edwards, and he was not eager to accept. His seven laborious years at Stockbridge had finally brought him a peaceful existence with the affection and respect of his neighbors; the friendship of two disciples, Bellamy and Hopkins, living close at hand; and ample leisure for the continuation of his study and writing. Also he may not have greatly relished the prospect of succeeding his son-in-law in the presidency. There is some evidence that Edwards had previously refused the post before Aaron Burr accepted it in 1748.

Before reaching a decision, Edwards gave the trustees an

honest appraisal of his feelings in a long letter arranged in formal fashion, almost like a sermon. He presented his weaknesses as a candidate, followed by his advantages; his reasons against accepting, followed by those in favor. Even the latter were half-hearted. First of all, he stood to lose financially. Having acquired a house and land at Stockbridge, guaranteeing him a "comfortable situation," he was afraid that the salary promised at Princeton would barely meet the expenses he would have to incur in order to support the prestige of his office. He had planned to spend the rest of his life in study and writing, his "chief entertainment and delight," activities which his new duties would probably curtail. But the most telling reasons for Edwards' hesitation lay in his personal defects, which he unflinchingly listed in a most revealing autobiographical passage, as dispassionate as a clinical report. "I have a constitution, in many respects, peculiarly unhappy, attended with flaccid solids, vapid, sizy, and scarce fluids, and a low tide of spirits; often occasioning a kind of childish weakness and contemptibleness of speech, presence, and demeanour, with a disagreeable dulness and stiffness, much unfitting one for conversation, but more especially for the government of a college." He was also deficient in several academic areas, including the higher mathematics and the Greek classics.

The foundation of his intellectual life, as he saw it, was his method of study, which consisted of note-taking and writing. Whenever he received a hint or clue to truth in reading, conversation, or meditation, he pursued it with his pen, setting forth his best thoughts on innumerable subjects for his own benefit. He regarded his life as a pleasant journey through a constantly enlarging field in which his chosen path entailed the exposing of the prevailing theological errors of his day. In addition to his previous peregrinations—his works on free will and original sin—he had projected an encyclopedic work to be called *History of the Work of Redemption,* "a body of divinity in an entirely new method, being thrown into the form of a history; considering the affair of Christian theology, as the whole of it in each part, stands in reference to the great work of redemption by Jesus Christ; which I suppose to be, of all others, the grand design of God, and the *summum* and *ultimum* of all the divine operations and decrees." In this

[62]

framework Edwards proposed to write the history of all three worlds, heaven, earth, and hell, "considering the connected, successive events and alterations in each, so far as the Scriptures give any light."

Edwards' heart was so much in this work that he could not conscientiously commit himself to an academic load as heavy as that which Burr had formerly carried, instructing in all the languages and teaching the entire program for one of the classes in addition to administrative duties. Edwards was willing to carry out the supervisory activities of the president; oversee all the instruction; teach when necessary, especially the senior class; and in addition undertake "the whole work of a professor of divinity, in public and private lectures." In comparison with the duties of other colonial college presidents, this was a light load. In a sense, Edwards was presenting his terms, but still he would not promise to accept even if they were granted. He must first ask the advice of his "most wise, friendly, and faithful" counselors and secure the consent of the Boston commissioners.

Before coming to his decision about Princeton, Edwards received a touching letter from his widowed daughter describing her affliction and the state of her soul. One of her sons had also been stricken with fever and had come near to death, but her tribulation had taught her that her children were not her own but God's. Her great theme—as was her father's as well as that of the deists—was "I cannot doubt but all is for the best." But, unlike the deists, the Edwardses received assurance through transport. Esther Burr saw the kind of visions her father had described in his "Personal Narrative." During the time when God called her to give up her child, her soul had been exalted to "eager desires after perfection and the full enjoyment of God." "I think," she confided to her father, "I had that night a foretaste of heaven. . . . I slept but little, and when I did, my dreams were all of heavenly and divine things." Yet a few days later she was tormenting herself because of her sins, particularly that of pride, and the fancied darts of Satan. When she was about to renew her covenant with God, the doubts came to her mind: It is better not to renew than to renew and break the contract—and how did she know that God would help her to keep her covenant? "Oh, to be delivered," she agonized, "from the power of Satan, as well as sin!" It was hard to live on the Edwards plan. If one had no enthusiastic transports, one would seem not to be converted; if one experienced religious rapture, it could be attributed to the Devil—and the Devil seemed also to be responsible for the lethargy that followed such transports. Throughout his life Edwards subjected himself to endless spiritual scrutiny and torment.

In the first week of January, 1758, a formal meeting was held at Stockbridge, attended by Edwards' advisors and his congregation, to hear the offer from Princeton, Edwards' view of the situation, and the objections, if any, of his people. When all had had their say, the assemblage decided that it was Edwards' duty to accept. Edwards "fell into tears" and remarked that "it was matter of wonder to him, that they could so easily . . . get over the objections he had made against his removal." Probably he was somewhat miffed that they had added no objections of their own.

Shortly after arriving in Princeton, Edwards heard that his father had died on January 27, at the age of eighty-nine. In less than three months Edwards was to join him.

The first sermon he preached at Princeton, on the unchangeable nature of Christ, took more than two hours in delivery. He subsequently preached other sermons, but his only teaching consisted in listening to seniors recite assigned topics in divinity.

Since a number of cases of smallpox had broken out in Princeton, Edwards, Esther Burr, and her children were all inoculated on February 13, but unfortunately they were thus given the disease instead of being protected against later attacks. Edwards died on March 22, at the age of fifty-five, and his daughter passed away two weeks after him.

Edwards had once observed that a saint who is ripe for heaven easily quits this world. When he learned that his symptoms were fatal, however, the comfortable part of his philosophy of gloomy optimism deserted him for a brief moment. He could not comprehend "the meaning of this mysterious conduct of Providence, in calling him out from his beloved privacy, to a public scene of action and influence; and then so suddenly, just upon his entrance into it, transforming him from thence, in such a way, by mortality." But his theology of a lifetime almost immediately overpowered his doubts, and he once again yielded to his faith in the sovereignty of divine providence.

Edwards' doctor was William Shippen, a physician at the Pennsylvania Hospital and one of the most eminent medical men in Philadelphia, who had been brought to Princeton expressly for the inoculation. At Edwards' bedside at the end, Shippen wrote a circumstantial letter of condolence to the widow. "Never did any mortal man more fully and clearly evidence the sincerity of all his professions, by one continued, universal, calm, cheerful resignation, and patient submission to the Divine will, through every stage of his disease, than he; not so much as one discontented expression, nor the least appearance of murmuring, through the whole. And never did any person expire with more perfect freedom from pain; —not so much as one distorted hair—but in the most proper sense of the words, he fell asleep. Death had certainly lost its sting, as to him."

As he neared death, Edwards' finest humanitarian qualities came to the fore. He expressly ordered his daughter Lucy to see that the expenses of his funeral, like that of his son-in-law, should be kept to the minimum and that the money so saved be "disposed of to charitable uses." Edwards' theology made him at times talk against human benevolence, but all evidence indicates that he epitomized that virtue in his life.

Edwards' passing was given scant attention in the colonial press. Even the Boston papers had no more than a line or two, except the *Gazette*, which printed a short paragraph on April 10. The only extensive notice, surprisingly enough, appeared in Benjamin Franklin's *Pennsylvania Gazette* on April 6. Gilbert Tennent contributed a letter, which has never been reprinted, dramatically describing Edwards' last moments. "When eternity drew near, he, with undisturbed composure, desired his daughter to request her mother, and his wife, not to indulge excessive grief . . . but to consider, that the spiritual relation between them would not be dissolved by death, and that he hoped to see her again. And likewise that she should tell the other children, that he requested them to observe the instructions he had from time to time given them, and that if they did so, good would come to them. After he had spoken to the above purpose, he looked about, and said, 'Now, where is Jesus of Nazareth, my true and never failing

[65]

friend?' And so he fell asleep, and went to that Lord he loved."

Tennent's estimate of Edwards' achievement was about as high as anyone's at that time:

> A person of great eminence, both in respect of capacity, learning, piety and usefulness; a good scholar, and a great divine. As his genius was extraordinary, so it was greatly improved by long and hard study, by which he treasured up much useful knowledge, both divine and human, and was thus uncommonly prepared for the arduous and important province to which he was called. Divinity was his favourite study, in the knowledge of which he had few, if any, equals, and no superior in these provinces. The humility, gravity and modesty of his behaviour rendered him amiable to all that feared God, who had the pleasure and privilege of his acquaintance. But nothing appeared with greater lustre, and more striking charms in his conduct, than his candor to man and his fidelity to his God. . . . His judicious and magnanimous defence of the principles of the Christian reformed religion, against the plausible pretexts and cavils of Arminians, in a late volume upon the liberty of the human will (a volume, in which their cause is with great force of argument entirely baffled; and it is thought by some professors of divinity in Europe, and by divers divines here, that it exceeds any thing that has been wrote on the subject) and his excellent writings in behalf of the power of piety (which some time since happily spread in this sinful land) deserve esteem, and will make his memory blossom in the dust.

After more in the same strain, Tennent concluded with a geographically inaccurate apostrophe: "*O* Prince-Town, *the Beauty of* Israel *is slain upon thy high Places!*"

Chapter 2

EXISTENCE *PER SE*

In tracing Edwards' intellectual development, we must recognize that his initial, constant, and dominating influence was that of New England theology, which he inherited from his parents along with his gaunt physical stature. By New England theology, we mean the Christian Scriptures, Calvinistic doctrine as interpreted by colonial ministers, and local notions of church government.

Even though Edwards in turn helped to construct this same theology and stamped it to some extent with his own thought, it was the primary influence upon his mind ever since the age of five when he erected his woodland prayer house. When, as a student at Yale, he later plunged into the thought of Newton and Locke, he was already so imbued with his religion that it was inevitable that he establish his personal philosophy as an attempt to reconcile with his views of the Scripture the physical discoveries of Newton and the psychological theories of Locke.

The most abstruse and conjectural part of Edwards' philosophical system is the first he formulated—his concept of ontology, entitled "Of Being" in his Notes on Natural Science.

Edwards' first principle is the necessary and eternal existence of infinite and omnipresent being, a principle which he regarded as self-evident. This eternal being cannot be solid, he reasoned, for solidity is nothing but resistance to other solids; therefore "space is this necessary, eternal, infinite and omnipresent being." Our reason, Edwards argued, confirms this principle. We can easily imagine the nonexistence of any other being, but we cannot conceive of the nonexistence of space. So far in his reasoning Edwards would meet with little opposition. His next step, however, establishes his individual bias. "I had as good speak plain," he announced; "I have already said as much as that space is God." Edwards' notion of space comprises all which is not proper to body, all the space beyond the confines of creation, and all the space before creation.

It is equally self-evident, he affirmed, that being is conscious, since "consciousness and being are the same thing exactly." It grated upon Edwards' mind "to think that something should be from all eternity, and nothing all the while be conscious of it," but others may find it equally unwarranted to assume as he does that consciousness and being are identical. Edwards attempted a demonstration, however, by supposing the creation of another universe of excellent order and harmony inhabited by nothing but insentient bodies. If nothing but God knew anything of this world, Edwards concluded, it could have no being but in divine consciousness. Actually this supposition proves merely that consciousness is necessary for existence to be perceived—not that God is space. Some Christian philosophers of Edwards' day had argued that the principles of beauty and good existed independently of God and that the divine being conformed to these independent ideas when he created the universe. It would be no more of an absurdity to believe that the entire universe could exist without God. The atheists, moreover, firmly maintained the eternity of the world—a position philosophically as respectable as the view that the world was created.

To Edwards, the only possible objection to his theory that consciousness is necessary to existence would be that it amounts to the same thing as supposing that a room which is shut up so that nobody can look inside is therefore nonexistent. Such a supposition is indeed a weighty objection, not really invalidated by Edwards' reply that some created beings might eventually have some consciousness of the room, "for perhaps there is not one leaf of a tree nor spire of grass but what has effects all over the universe, and will have to the end of eternity." This statement may be true, but it is really not to the purpose of proving that nothing may exist without consciousness. Edwards still maintained that, except for these long-range effects, "there is nothing in a room shut up but only in God's consciousness." Indeed, he insisted, if all the spirits in the world were suddenly deprived of consciousness and the consciousness of God were intermitted, "the universe for that time would cease to be, of itself."

The direct source of Edwards' theory of consciousness—in turn the basis of his idealism—was Locke's demonstration that colors are not in the objects themselves but in the eye of the person who perceives them. As we know, Locke came to this conclusion by making an analogy with the color-blind person who cannot perceive colors. Locke did not suggest that if everyone were blind and incapable of touch, there would be no rational universe, but Edwards extended his own principle of subjectivism to this point. He argued that if there were no light to enable us to see and at the same time no motion in the universe, the universe would be tantamount to a void. There would be no shape, color, noise, solidity, magnitude, proportion, heat or cold, wet or dry, hard or soft. The universe would then exist only in the divine mind.

Unlike Locke, Edwards affirmed that for him there was no more reason for anything in body to have existence apart from the mind than for color to have existence apart from the mind. To rid the world of its material existence, Edwards attacked in his argument the notion of solidity, which he argued can be nothing else but "resistance to touch, the resistance of some parts of space." Since one body cannot resist another without motion, he concluded that a world without motion can exist only in the mind.

God is basic in all parts of Edwards' philosophy—and all parts tend to demonstrate the existence of God. To his spiritual argument that existence in itself implies consciousness, he added a physical argument based on the atomic theory, defining an atom as a *minimum physicum,* a body which cannot be made less, and assuming that all larger bodies in the universe are made up of atoms. Since everything in the universe is composed of atoms, he maintained, there must be an infinite force or power to bring them together and keep them touching. This infinite power is God. Since such an infinite power is needed to keep bodies in being, Edwards affirmed, there must have been an infinite power to bring them into being; the world could not have existed from eternity, as the atheists allege, but must have been created by a divine being. Moreover since body is nothing but an infinite resistance in some part of space through the immediate exercise of divine power, every minute of existence is actually as marvelous as the first minute of the creation, when, as Edwards rhapsodically expressed it, that wonderful work was performed "which was seen by the morning stars when they sang together."

To Edwards, creation of the corporeal universe was nothing but the first causing of resistance in space, with a power of continuing this resistance afterwards under identical conditions. This principle explains at the same time the laws of nature in bodies.

If we accept the view that body and solidity are the same and that resistance represents the immediate exercise of the divine power, we need not assume the existence of any real substance or property belonging to bodies as such. Contrary to "Hobbes's notion that God is matter and that all substance is matter," Edwards affirmed that "nothing that is matter can possibly be God and that no matter is, in the most proper sense (of a self-subsisting substance) matter." There is, therefore, no such thing as mechanism in the sense of bodies acting each upon another purely and properly by themselves, but there is a divinely instituted and divinely supported mechanism.

Edwards had no difficulty in reconciling an atomic theory and the physical laws of Newton to his idealistic system, in which only spirit has real existence and according to which matter is an illusion of the senses. He held, for example, that the things which are objects of seeing are merely mental existences in the same way that objects in a mirror have no real existence but exist only mentally. Nothing belonging to body, Edwards insisted, exists out of the mind except "resistance, which is solidity; and the termination of this resistance with its relations, which is figure; and the communication of the resistance from space to space, which is motion." And since all of these modes are forms of resistance, and resistance is nothing but the exertion of God's power, this resistance cannot exist out of the mind—one more way of proving the world to be an ideal one.

If we assume that the universe has existence only in God's mind and that our perceptions give us insight only into an ideal world, we are faced with the problem of how God's

ideas and our ideas coexist, that is, how our ideas conform
with those of God. Edwards' explanation is merely an extension of his theory of God's active participation in the
corporeal world through resistance. In things that are supposed to be without us, Edwards affirmed, truth is "the determination and fixed mode of God's exciting ideas in us."
God and real existence are the same, and God has contrived
an agreement of our ideas with his own. In this connection,
Edwards remarked, in a sober play on words, upon the great
propriety of the names of the deity: Jehovah, and "I am that
I am"—another way of saying that God is existence.

To say that the material universe "exists nowhere but in
the mind," Edwards cautioned, does not suggest that an individual human body and brain exist materially and comprehend the rest of the universe within them. The brain exists
only mentally, in exactly "the same sense that other things
do." The philosophy of idealism does not "deny that things
are where they seem to be" nor does it "make void natural
philosophy, or the science of the causes or reasons of corporeal
changes." Even though "the existence of the whole material
universe is absolutely dependent on idea, yet we may speak
in the old way, and as properly and truly as ever." Atoms
are merely ideas in God's mind, but they have as real an
existence as though they were material. God has determined
that these ideas shall be united forever in a connected and
coordinated series. And "all the ideas that ever were or ever
shall be to all eternity in any created mind are answerable
to the existence of such a peculiar atom in the beginning of
the creation of such a determinate figure and size, and having
such a motion given it." Even though no human mind may
perceive any atom or group of atoms united in activity, God
by supposing their existence "causes all changes to arise as if
all these things had actually existed in such a series in some
created mind." Perhaps the clearest view of Edwards' idealism
comes in his distinction between the material universe and
the spirits which perceive it. "When I say, the material universe exists only in the mind, I mean that it is absolutely dependent on the conception of the mind for its existence, and
does not exist as spirits do, whose existence does not consist
in, nor in dependence on, the conception of other minds."
Presumably the spirits Edwards refers to may be either human

beings or angels. Human beings would consequently have an independent existence as perceiving beings, but at the same time be part of the material universe for other beings.

Solidity, Edwards admitted, is essential to physical being, for "if solidity be removed from body nothing is left but empty space." And according to his theory that resistance is the constant exertion of God's power, "solidity or impenetrability is as much action, or the immediate result of action, as gravity." This conclusion led Edwards to his own version of a proof of the existence of God based on gravity—a form of reasoning which Newton had originally used in letters to Bentley and which the latter had publicized in a famous series of sermons against atheism. Since gravity is obviously the result of some active influence, there must have been some agent which set bodies in motion. Similarly there must be some active influence to stop a body already in motion or "to stop all motion at the limits of such and such parts of space." If we are justified in attributing the cause of gravity to God, Edwards reasoned, we are equally justified in attributing the action by which we gain the idea of solidity to the same divine source. The latent quality which upholds the properties of bodies, is, therefore, according to Edwards, not the ambiguous "substance" of the materialists, but God or that "He 'by whom all things consist.' "

"The secret lies here," Edwards affirmed, "that which truly is the Substance of all Bodies, is the infinitely exact, and precise, and perfectly stable Idea, in God's mind, together with his stable Will, that the same shall gradually be communicated to us, and to other minds, according to certain fixed and exact established Methods and Laws." This hypothesis may have satisfied Edwards; it is actually no more profound than that of the Indian philosopher who revealed that the frame of the world is supported by a huge elephant and then, when he was pressed a little further, explained that the elephant is in turn borne up by a huge tortoise.

Edwards himself in a later work, *Miscellaneous Observations on Important Theological Subjects,* formulated one of the major objections to idealism—that the sense organs, which give us ideas, have themselves no independent existence but exist only in the mind, for they are part of the sensible world. "And then it will follow, that the organs of sense owe their existence to the organs of sense, and so are prior to themselves, being the causes or occasions of their own existence; which is a seeming inconsistence with reason."

Another difficulty in Edwards' theological idealism is that it attributes absolutely everything in the universe to the constant support and activity of God. Most psychological and physiological phenomena such as memory, emotion, and metabolism can be explained as processes quite independent of a divine stimulus. Why must we assume a divine influence in everything merely to justify it in some things? Edwards' hypothesis raises more questions than it solves: for example, how is God's consciousness communicated to the individual consciousness, and how is one separated from the other? As Bolingbroke replied to Berkeley's theories of grace, "should a word be invented to signify a moral cause of effects purely physical, or a physical cause of effects purely moral, you would laugh at the invention and you would be in the right." Many philosophers who believe in God feel that there is a truth about the universe which can be explained without recourse to God at all points. And many other philosophers completely reject the being of God. For these reasons, Edwards' theory has few adherents. Edwards himself endorsed Philip Skelton's admission that if it were not for divine revelation, natural reason would lead us to be materialists and Manichaeans.

Chapter 3

RELIGIOUS AFFECTIONS

Edwards' first major work, his *Treatise concerning Religious Affections*, which has been more widely read than anything else he ever wrote, is generally considered important for its analysis of the structure of the mind. Edwards wrote it for the benefit of common minds perplexed by the upheavals of the Great Awakening as well as for his fellow divines, and he included "for the sake of the more illiterate reader" such aids as a simple distinction between natural and moral evil. In vindicating the free expression of emotion in religion, Edwards was not actually a pioneer. He had been preceded by the Cambridge Platonists and by Lord Shaftesbury's *Letter concerning Enthusiasm*. But instead of adopting the arguments they had advanced based on social utility or inventing others based on the therapeutic value of the exercise of all natural faculties, Edwards typically demonstrated that since the emotions are held up in the Scriptures as instruments for praise, worship, and communication with God, they must be accepted and esteemed.

There was indeed much good that Edwards could say about emotional religion, and his enemies had already said much that was bad. Edwards shrugged off most of their criticism by blaming Satan for all the absurd and tragic results of the emotional exhibitionism which religion engenders. The treatise on the affections is the only one of Edwards' works in which Satan plays a major part. Even in the notorious Enfield sermon, it is sinners in the hands of an angry God—not of a malicious Devil. In Edwards' treatises on excellence, beauty, and virtue, he says very little about Satan or why he was created. In all his works we find no systematic explanation of evil in the universe, not even in his treatise on original sin, where one would naturally expect to find it. Most theological systems are embarrassed when they attempt to account for evil. Edwards was particularly vulnerable to the charge of laying evil to the divine account because of his ontology, which finds God present in absolutely everything in the universe. As a matter of fact, Edwards in his treatise on the will argued himself into admitting that, to all intents and purposes, God is responsible for sin. Yet he was obviously reluctant to accept the implications of his admission. Like the deists, Edwards was so convinced of the benevolence of the universe that he frequently forgot that part of it is imperfect and thus lost sight of his doctrinal conviction of the corruptness of the human race.

Edwards divided the soul or human personality into two parts, the understanding and the inclinations, a dichotomy which exists in Calvinism as understanding and will. Edwards taught that the understanding—more generally called the mind—carries on perception and speculation, discernment, and judging. The inclinations or affections—more generally called the heart—engage in liking or disliking, in feeling pleasure or displeasure. The violent affections in this system are the passions. True religion, he maintained, consists in large measure in holy affections, which, in common with the other affections, are "no other than the more vigorous and sensible exercises of the inclination and will of the soul."

The essence of Edwards' argument is that religion requires love of God rather than mere assent to the proposition that he exists. "If we be not in good earnest in religion," he affirmed, "and our wills and inclinations be not strongly exercised, we are nothing." Edwards' emphasis on the affections as instruments of attachment to a spiritual force outside the individual has more than a surface resemblance to the existentialist concept of "engagement." Edwards insisted: "He that has doctrinal knowledge and speculation only, without affection, never is *engaged* in the business of religion." Edwards' emphasis on total dedication foreshadows the doctrine of his last major treatises, in which he defines true virtue as love to being in general. In these works, love, not perception or understanding, is seen as the essence of true religion or true virtue. Edwards really makes no distinction between religion and virtue. But if there is no true religion without affection, neither can there be true religion where there is nothing else but affection. True love to God, as Edwards makes abundantly clear, will have its side effects in personal rectitude, love to fellow beings, and good works. For Edwards, the ethical principle was almost taken for granted, one reason that it was highly important in his daily life but not stressed in his doctrine.

After setting forth his psychological theory of the affections and demonstrating that they are an inherent part of religious experience, Edwards took up the problem of determining the relationship between particular emotional reactions in individuals and their state of grace; in other words, whether external behavior indicates a certainty of salvation. He first described a number of psychological phenomena which are neither signs that the individual possesses the grace of God nor signs that he does not. For example, it is no indication one way or the other if the emotions are raised to a high pitch or if they result in violent effects in the body. Edwards particularly observed that no set order of emotional reaction progressing from distress to comfort and joy is necessary for conversion. We remember that Edwards was perplexed in his own religious experience because he had not gone through the stages prescribed by most divines. He comforted and encouraged the saints of his own flock by assuring them that they were saved, but in his treatise he affirmed that no assurance given by a second party can have any validity. "The true saints have not such a spirit of discerning, that they can certainly determine who are godly, and who are not. For though they know experimentally what true religion is, in the internal exercise of it; yet these are what they can neither feel nor see, in the heart of another."

Although some emotional responses may be caused as well by the Devil as by the Holy Spirit, and although an outsider may not be able infallibly to detect the internal state of a fellow believer, Edwards argued that it is, nevertheless, possible to recognize certain signs which distinguish "truly gracious and holy affections." Most of these are of such a personal nature that an outside observer would need to be extremely acute to perceive them. Edwards believed that genuine gracious affections are grounded in love of the divine excellence of God and Christ in both natural and moral manifestations.

These affections bring enlightenment to the mind, enabling it to understand divine things, not as doctrinal acquiescence but through perception of spiritual beauty. "There arises from this sense of spiritual beauty, all true experimental knowledge of religion, which is of itself as it were a new world of knowledge."

Edwards gave this process a psychological basis by assuming the existence of a separate sense, a sense of holiness, parallel to the sense of beauty and to the many other senses which Francis Hutcheson had previously added to the conventional five senses. Edwards, however, in support of his theory that external beauty, harmony in music, or good food may be recognized immediately without the need of reasoning about them, cited the article "Taste" in Ephraim Chambers' *Cyclopædia*, a reference work that Edwards used extensively. By affirming the existence of an internal sense of spiritual beauty, Edwards was assenting to a concept of intuitive knowledge quite alien to the empiricism of Locke, his usual authority for psychological matters.

Edwards gave a twofold character to his process of intuition. The primary characteristic, a divine illumination or apprehension of spiritual things, has its effects entirely in the feelings; the secondary characteristic, a conviction of the reality and certainty of divine things, has its effects in the intellect. The person who receives this conviction has no doubts whatsoever concerning the truth of the doctrines of the gospel. His supernatural sense has furnished him with "direct, clear, and all-conquering evidence."

For Edwards, therefore, there are three ways of being persuaded of the truth of the Christian religion: (1) that based upon emotion alone, which gives the person an illusion of divine discoveries, but leaves him with no real sight of the truth; (2) that based upon natural reason, from which the person derives merely mental assent or belief; and (3) that based upon spiritual illumination, which combines emotional pleasure from perceiving the truth with a rational conviction of certainty. Edwards compared this intuitive understanding of the doctrines of Christianity to a refined taste in literature: "Those things in Milton, which to mean judges appear tasteless and imperfections, are his inimitable excellencies in the eyes of those who are of greater discerning, and better taste."

[77]

The other results of gracious affections which Edwards enumerated have a more ethical than psychological significance. These affections give the Christian a sense of "his own utter insufficiency, despicableness, and odiousness"; change his nature by releasing him from absolute domination by his sins; promote humility, meekness, and tenderness of spirit; exalt the desire for greater spiritual attainments; and are exercised and bear fruit in Christian practice or good works. Maintaining an esthetic parallel, Edwards insisted that the gracious affections differ from the false in their "beautiful symmetry and proportion." By this he meant that the saints show their love to all people at all times and places instead of exhibiting partiality and eccentricity, and that they give their attention to the virtues of their fellow Christians and to their own defects, rather than the reverse.

Although some modern critics have felt that Edwards stresses the "primacy of the aesthetic element over the moral and legal," this judgment cannot be supported in the totality of Edwards' writings. Like the Platonists, Edwards tended to merge the esthetic and the moral, and frequently when he seems to be dealing with esthetic concepts—as in the discussion of the "beautiful symmetry and proportion" of the affections—he is really describing patterns of behavior. The ethical element is strong in Edwards, as Benjamin Franklin recognized many years ago, although it is not strange that modern critics should neglect it. For those who study Edwards' philosophy, it is more interesting to write about his metaphysics than his practical ethics—and more people study Edwards' philosophy than study his principles of conduct. But it is almost misrepresenting him to ignore such passages as the following from *Religious Affections:* "In order to men's being true Christians, it is necessary that they prosecute the business of religion, and the service of God, with great earnestness and diligence, as the work to which they devote themselves, and make the main business of their lives. All Christ's *peculiar people,* not only do good works, but are *zealous of good works.*"

Edwards insisted that Christian practice is not only "the greatest evidence that *others* can have of the sincerity of a professing Christian," but also the chief sign to the individual himself. As John E. Smith expressed it, "It is no small irony that a skillful and vigorous defense of the primacy of practice in religion should have found expression in a treatise on religious *affections.*" Edwards anticipated two major objections to this doctrine from those of his contemporaries who disliked a gospel of good works: (1) that experience should be the paramount rule by which to judge grace, and (2) that the emphasis on practice seemed to overturn the doctrine of justification by faith in favor of justification by works. To the first objection Edwards replied that there should be no distinction between Christian experience and practice. "Holy practice is one kind of Christian experience; and both reason and Scripture represent it as the chief, and most important, and most distinguishing part of it." To the second objection Edwards answered that it does not in any sense "diminish the honour and importance of faith, that its exercises and effects in practice should be esteemed its chief signs; any more than it lessens the importance of life, that action and motion are esteemed its chief signs."

Ordinarily one cannot make great claims about Edwards' literary style, but the treatise on the affections contains one passage of great beauty—an almost lyrical expression of calm assurance:

> . . . All who are truly religious are not of this world, they are strangers here, and belong to heaven; they are born from above, heaven is their native country, and the nature which they receive by this heavenly birth, is a heavenly nature, they receive an anointing from above; that principle of true religion which is in them, is a communication of the religion of heaven; their grace is the dawn of glory; and God fits them for that world by conforming them to it.

With unaggressive complacence, Edwards deliberately contrasted his mystical Religion of Heaven with the deists' abstract Religion of Nature.

Chapter 4

THE WILL

The concept of God-intoxication—originally developed by Philo and subsequently associated with Spinoza—has equal reference to Edwards, the thinker. Of course, Edwards himself would not have admitted that he had anything in common with Spinoza. Indeed he once specifically disclaimed pantheism by insisting that God is "an intelligent, wise agent, that presides, not as the soul of the world, but as the Sovereign Lord of the universe." Yet Edwards conceived of God as the prime mover and immanent force in every material and spiritual phenomenon. Going beyond the vague spirit in which most theologians would accept this premise, Edwards made it concrete, conceiving of God's immediate presence or manifestation in every object or movement in the universe. In Edwards' scheme, God is the heart of the material universe. At the same time he controls every thought and deed of every creature in the universe. Nothing is governed by chance; nothing is provisional in either the physical or moral world.

In his theology of salvation, moreover, Edwards embraced those doctrines which attribute power and goodness to God rather than to man. This point was the basic issue between Calvinists and Arminians. The latter, by their doctrines of freedom of will and limited grace, granted man some choice in his behavior—in whether he would be virtuous or evil and whether he would accept or reject the plan of salvation. But the Calvinistic doctrines of necessity, efficacious grace, and absolute, eternal, personal election ascribed everything to God, nothing to man.

The work upon which Edwards' greatest fame rests, *Freedom of the Will*, contains little "pure" philosophy such as we find in his notebooks. He considered the theological aspects of the question more important than the psychological or ontological—and much of his theology is on the level of polemic rather than sincere inquiry. Yet Edwards felt called upon to apologize for his philosophical orientation. In most moral and theological controversy of the period, the disputants contrasted "philosophical and metaphysical arguments" with "common sense," and Edwards conformed to the tradition even while admitting that his fellow Calvinists had often been accused of running into "nice scholastic distinctions, and abstruse metaphysical subtleties." In his very first paragraph, he deprecated metaphysical refinements and blamed the philosophers and metaphysicians for the obscurity surrounding the matter of the will. Throughout the body of his work he inveighed in conventional rationalistic scorn against the unintelligibility of Duns Scotus and St. Thomas Aquinas, the indeterminate meanings of philosophical terms, and kindred "metaphysical niceties and subtleties." But in the midst of his treatise Edwards argued that metaphysics is a legitimate branch of inquiry and that "if the reasoning be good, 'tis as frivolous to inquire what science it is properly reduced to, as what language it is delivered in." Some subjects are inherently metaphysical, he maintained; for example, the being and nature of God. "We can have no proof, that is properly demonstrative, of any one proposition" relating to it which is not metaphysical. If a subject belongs to metaphysics, moreover, he argued, it does not follow that reasoning about it "must needs be abstruse, unintelligible, and akin to the jargon of the schools."

Despite Edwards' antimetaphysical disclaimers, his *Inquiry* is itself abstruse and intricate, but surprisingly enough it is least so in the section devoted to his formal proof of determinism, which occupies scarcely one-tenth of the entire work. We must remember that his primary purpose was not really to demonstrate necessity, but to demolish the contentions of the Arminian theologians that freedom of the will is "essential to moral agency, virtue and vice, reward and punishment, praise and blame." The bulk of the work is concerned with highly abstract ethical and teleological concepts rather than with practical psychology. The reader who is persuaded by Edwards' relatively simple major premise of determinism is likely to lose his conviction in the appended maze of controversy. This is perhaps an inevitable consequence of the doctrine itself. As Dr. Johnson once said, "All theory is against the freedom of the will, all experience for it."

In Edwards' day, a Don Juan convinced of materialistic necessity would nevertheless cultivate the arts of persuasion and practice all the devices of seduction, even though he might believe intellectually that necessity alone would determine whether his victims would succumb. And in our day, a deterministic atheist in a restaurant will hesitate between the onion soup and the consommé just as though he were not convinced that his decisions are irrevocably fixed in advance. Edwards himself became one of the leading evangelists of his age—appealing personally to individuals in his congregation to change their hearts and their conduct—at the same time that he privately believed that God predetermined every response.

Although Edwards wrote one mammoth treatise on the affections and another on the will, he believed that the will is virtually identical with the affections. In both treatises he declared that the affections are only certain modes of the exercise of the will.

Edwards' whole argument for necessity is based upon three interrelated principles: (1) the dominance of the strongest motive, (2) the chain of cause and effect, and (3) the distinction between natural and moral necessity. Virtually everything else in his treatise is a gloss upon these three.

Edwards' statement of the first of the above principles is clear and simple: "It is that motive, which, as it stands in the view of the mind, is the strongest, that determines the will." If we accept only this much, we need actually go no further to establish that the will is not free, for what seems to be the exercise of choice is merely determination by the strongest motive, even though it may not always be obvious or instantaneous. One does not need to be a philosopher to accept this principle. A character in one of Henry Fielding's novels, published three years before Edwards' *Inquiry*, maintained that "every man acted entirely from that passion which was uppermost." Edwards in his notes on the mind similarly affirmed that every creature automatically moves to secure his greatest happiness, for "the love of happiness is the same

[82]

with the faculty of the will." In the same discussion he re-marked: "The will, choice, etc., is nothing else but the mind's being pleased with an idea, or having a superior pleasedness in something thought of, or a desire of a future thing, . . . or a disagreeable conception of the contrary state at that time when we desire it." Locke had written that it is uneasiness in present circumstances which always determines the will, but Edwards argued that the will may have positive as well as purely negative reactions. For example, if a man be asked to leave a seat and move to another place, he may refuse to do so—in which case his refusal (which is as much an act of will as adhering to the request) is not in any way the result of uneasiness in present circumstances.

The second principle Edwards states with less clarity and directness than the first. It is the principle that every act of every individual will is part of a chain of cause and effect operating within that individual and at the same time also interconnected with every other activity in the universe. As the deist Anthony Collins had expressed it earlier in the century, men's actions "are so determin'd by the causes pre-ceding each action, that not one past action could possibly not have come to pass, or have been otherwise than it hath been; nor one future action can possibly not come to pass, or be otherwise than it shall be." When baldly stated, this doc-trine smacks of the ancient fatalists and the modern atheists, and it may be for this reason that Edwards shrouded it with ambiguities.

According to Joseph Priestley, Edwards was the first Calvinist to base determinism on cause and effect. In one of his notebooks, written before the age of thirty, Edwards set down the barren axiom: "Let this be laid down as a postulate before treating of those doctrines about free will: that what-ever is, there is some cause or reason why it is; and prove it." In his treatise Edwards declared that nothing ever comes to pass without a cause, using the word *cause* "to signify any antecedent, either natural or moral, positive or negative, on which an event, either a thing, or the manner and circum-stance of a thing, so depends, that it is the ground and reason, either in whole, or in part, why it is, rather than not; or why it is as it is, rather than otherwise." Edwards attempted no formal demonstration of the principle of causality, essential-

[83]

ly resting his case on describing it as "the grand principle of common sense." Without it, he affirmed, we could have no proof of any existence, not even of the being of God. We might still know of God's existence through intuition but we would have no means of proving it.

In his "Notes on the Mind" Edwards affirmed that we know intuitively that anything which begins to be or which undergoes any alteration must have a cause. "This is an innate principle, in that sense that the soul is born with it—a necessary, fatal propensity so to conclude, on every occasion." For this reason we know that any alteration in matter or spirit has a cause: for example, if a globe of solid matter hitherto at rest starts into motion, or if a spirit which has always had an inclination toward sin chooses holiness. Also the mind concludes that there is a cause for the manner in which something exists as well as for its mere being. The most complex and sublime illustration of the mind's intuition of causes is the perception of the beauty and contrivance of the world and the inevitable conclusion that "its cause was a being that had design." For Edwards, this way of assuming causation "is a sort of ratiocination."

Like Hume, Edwards rejected the old-fashioned notion of the efficient causation of one event by a preceding one in favor of the concept of constant conjunction. In other words, a chain of events may be conjoined one with another, without one event necessarily being the motivating force of a subsequent one. In his miscellanies, Edwards illustrated this notion of conjunction to distinguish it from the concept of efficient cause. God may decree that his people pray for rain and he may also decree that the rain fall immediately afterward, but the rain cannot be considered as a result of the prayers, nor the prayers an efficient cause of the rain.

The third principle, that concerning natural and moral necessity, has its roots in the thought of St. Augustine and Luther as well as in Hobbes. There are many occasions when we perform an action while being under no physical necessity to do so—when we have the choice to perform it or not: for example, to look to the left or to look to the right. According to the necessitarians, however, our will never has this freedom and always requires us to perform in a certain way. We have liberty of action within the limits of physical possibility, but we have no liberty of will. Hobbes gave the classic illustration of the doctrine: "Liberty and necessity are consistent: as in the water, that hath not only *liberty*, but a *necessity* of descending by the channel." Converted to human behavior, this means that a man could be physically free to perform an action and at the same time be determined by his volition to do it. Hobbes also remarked captiously that anyone who "cannot understand the difference between *free to do if he will*, and free *to will*, is not fit . . . to hear this controversy disputed." According to this distinction, I would not be under physical necessity to turn my head to the right, since there would be no material obstacle to prevent me from holding it still or turning in the opposite direction. But I would be under moral necessity to turn it to the right if my will—based on strongest motive and cause and effect—should so determine.

Edwards was not the first Calvinist to elaborate this principle. A dissenting divine, Joseph Truman, had published a treatise in the preceding century, *On Moral and Natural Impotency*, in which he anticipated essentially everything Edwards was to say on the distinction. As Edwards defined the terms, moral necessity is "that necessity of connection and consequence, which arises from such *moral causes*, as the strength of inclination, or motives, and the connection which there is in many cases between these, and such certain volitions and actions." Natural necessity is that which comes from the force of natural causes: for example, feeling pain when wounded, seeing when one's eyes are open, and falling through the air when there is nothing to support one's body. By means of this distinction, Edwards obviously had no difficulty in supporting Hobbes's paradox that necessity is not inconsistent with liberty. Just as the water is both free to fall (in the sense of having no obstruction) and is also under the necessity of falling, so a man could be physically free to raise his arm and at the same time be under the moral necessity (through strongest motive) of raising it.

One might consider as a fourth independent principle a concept depending on the chain of cause and effect, but one which Edwards raises to a position of strategic significance: the principle that God's ordering of all events in the universe in itself requires complete and absolute necessity.

Edwards does not directly phrase this concept as such, but implies it in discussing a related notion, specifically, that God's certain foreknowledge of the future volition of moral agents is inconsistent with any degree of freedom. He points out that the exploits of a man such as Julius Caesar, which have had obvious consequences upon the subsequent destiny of mankind, themselves depended upon millions of acts of volition of his parents, which in turn depended upon millions of acts of their contemporaries and upon many more millions in preceding generations. Even the biological act of generation, the impregnating of the ovum by the masculine sperm, "must depend on things infinitely minute, relating to the time and circumstances of the act of the parents, the state of their bodies, etc. which must depend on innumerable foregoing circumstances and occurrences." God knew and arranged Caesar's birth and his conquest of the world. Pope had said the same thing in his *Essay on Man*, an unusual example of the poet preceding the philosopher:

> Who knows but he, whose hand the lightning forms,
> Who heaves old Ocean, and who wings the storms;
> Pours fierce Ambition in a Caesar's mind,
> Or turns young Ammon loose to scourge mankind?

As a further instance of the chain of cause and effect, Edwards affirmed that God was in direct control even when the successor to an empire had been chosen by an agreement that the candidate whose horse should neigh first after a particular hour would be the next ruler. And as concrete evidence of God's certain foreknowledge of the volition of moral agents, Edwards cited from both the Old and the New Testaments scores of instances of divine prophecies and their fulfillment. It is worth noting that Edwards did not use scriptural authority in his proofs of necessity as such—nor did he even introduce, until his concluding chapter, the doctrines of election and perseverance of the saints—but he drew freely upon Scripture to defend his corollary arguments such as this one of God's foreknowledge. The Arminians also accepted the notion of divine foreknowledge but denied that it was linked to personal or moral necessity; Edwards argued that it could be possible only through a chain of cause and effect, which implies necessity.

Chapter 5

ASSAULT ON ARMINIANS

An important part of Edwards' strategy in attempting to demolish the intellectual respectability of Arminianism was
based on semantic distinctions. He bluntly accused his opponents of changing the accepted meaning of language.
Liberty, in the ordinary usage of the word, he affirmed, means
simply the power and opportunity to do as one chooses without taking into consideration the cause of that choice, but
the Arminians have laden the word with several concepts
which only they accept. To them, liberty rests in a self-determining power of the will—a power which the will is said
to exercise over itself. They also maintained that the will must
be indifferent previous to an act of volition and that contingence must exist in every act—in the sense of there being
no foreseeable connection with any prior ground or condition.
According to the Arminians, moreover, virtue depends upon
making a choice, and there can be no moral agency without
this type of freedom. Thus virtue is the prevalence of good
over evil in a choice based on indifference and contingence.
To Edwards, however, virtue is the prevalence of good over
evil in a previously established predilection. Self-determination to the Arminians is a power which the will is said to
exercise over itself; it is, in other words, a power and a
faculty. To Edwards, the will itself is the power and nothing
else but a power.

The notion of self-determination Edwards considered as the
prime and indispensable tenet of the Arminian system. If this
could be overthrown, he felt, the entire system would be
undermined. He attacked the notion by trying to prove that
it rests upon an inner contradiction. His argument runs on
for pages of complicated syllogisms and conclusions, in a style

so involved that the thread is almost impossible to retain. Yet it can be simply stated: When the will makes a choice, it is really choosing to choose in a certain way, and this choice implies an antecedent choice. In other words, one can always go back one step behind the choice which seems to be self-determined. As Paul Ramsey has expressed it: "There is an act of the will determining what it shall choose, before the first act of choice; which is as much as to say, that there is an act of volition before the first act of volition." It is obviously a contradiction for an antecedent act to be supposed in an act which is self-determined. The first critic to reply to Edwards remarked that his "reasoning on self-determination may be well summed up thus: Because a man cannot take the second step without the first; therefore he cannot take the first without a previous one." Edwards' refutation of self-determinism is probably the least concrete and, according to some scholars, the least convincing of his assaults on the Arminians.

Edwards revealed the importance he attached to this single doctrine in his later work on original sin. He was ready to admit to the modern divines that "if they can maintain their peculiar notion of *freedom,* consisting in the *self-determining power of the will,* as necessary to *moral agency,* and can thoroughly establish it in opposition to the arguments lying against it, then they have an impregnable castle, to which they may repair, and remain invincible, in all the controversies they have with reformed divines, concerning Original Sin, the sovereignty of grace, election, redemption, conversion, the efficacious operation of the Holy Spirit, the nature of saving faith, perseverance of the saints, and other principles of like kind." He added that the same doctrine would be as strong a fortress for the deists. The doctrine was "almost inconceivably pernicious," Edwards felt, because it seemed to exculpate the individual from sin. He charged that even the most inveterate evil-doer will not admit that he has chosen his sin, but will fall back on the excuse that moral necessity required his lapses from virtue. Edwards actually argued in this fashion, even though this reasoning would seem to militate with as much force against his own more-embracing determinism. According to his reasoning, sinners who subscribe to any of the "kind of infidel schemes" based on the notion of free will or self-determination secretly blame God for their wickedness, not being instructed in the fundamental truth that *"a bad will, or an evil disposition of heart itself, is wickedness."* They recognize the hardness of their hearts, but vainly hope that this will count in their favor, justifying themselves in their inability. "Thus the strength of sin, is made the excuse for sin."

Obviously, if sin be divided into the two categories which Edwards set forth, the original hardness of heart inherent in the race of man and the particular acts of evil which spring from it, the second is negligible compared to the first. By writing off the first kind on the grounds of inability, the Arminian—in his own way of thinking—is then left with only the relatively insignificant kind. This he attempts to diminish in similar fashion by counting and magnifying his righteous acts, which he considers as having merit in his favor because they are self-determined. Thus the Arminian sinner allows his conscience to take him back to "the first wrong determination of the will, in some bad conduct," a small matter, and allows himself to forget his wickedness of heart. If self-determination is necessary for merit, the doctrine of imputed righteousness from Christ disappears altogether; for what is imputed from another, according to Edwards, does not result from our self-determination or our own action.

In this scheme of things, virtue is merely the piling up of self-determined good acts instead of the expression of the imputed righteousness of Christ, and sin is merely the piling up of self-determined evil acts. Salvation then seems to be within any man's power and an act of his own doing rather than God's—and sin is reduced to something inconsequential.

The factors of contingence and indifference were equally necessary to the Arminian scheme, but Edwards inveighed less strenuously against them, since they had virtually no theological implications, neither adding to nor diminishing man's importance in relation to God.

Contingence is the quality which, the Arminians maintained, exists in an event when that event "has absolutely no previous ground or reason, with which its existence has any fixed and certain connection." Edwards insisted that such events could not exist in either the moral or the natural world, since all events have a cause, and an event with a cause cannot be contingent.

According to the Arminians, indifference exists when the will is confronted with two or more choices and has absolutely no preference for one more than another. Edwards refuted this definition as he had that of self-determination, by charging it with being self-contradictory. To say that the mind can do as it pleases when it is indifferent "is to say that it can follow its pleasure when it has no pleasure to follow."

Edwards felt that the Arminian system was inconsistent in holding that we are not to be blamed for our evil but are to be rewarded for our good. His own system is certainly subject to the same criticism of logical imbalance—but in reverse. He held that we are condemned for our evil, but that our good will serve us for nothing, since we are actually incapable of good in an absolute sense; what seems to be good is good only relatively.

It is somewhat odd that Edwards should hold it against the Arminians that their system excuses man's evil deeds on the grounds of moral necessity, since this was exactly the argument used most widely against his own system and with more relevance. If the Arminians appealed to moral necessity to excuse some deeds, they certainly believed that others were free and subject to judgment. But Edwards argued that nothing was undetermined and that no human motivation could be wholesome. If the Arminian system is pernicious by giving the sinner an easy way out, the Calvinistic system seems equally pernicious by giving him no escape whatsoever. As Edwards' opponents alleged, the sinner only becomes hardened in his sin if he is convinced that he is irrevocably committed to it.

Actually both doctrines can be twisted so as to free all men from responsibility for their behavior. As a modern philosopher, Austin E. Duncan-Jones, has expressed it: "If the particular decision that I make, within a certain range, is not determined, then my previous life might have had the precise character that it actually had and I might none the less have made a different decision: I am therefore not responsible for having made this precise decision. And so on. A fortiori, unrestricted indifference is inconsistent with responsibility. We therefore have a simple constructive dilemma. If determinism is true, people are not responsible, and if the liberty of indifference is true, people are not responsible; but either determinism or the liberty of indifference is true; therefore people are not responsible."

Similarly, determinism could be accommodated to both deism and Christianity and is not a natural defense of orthodoxy as Edwards suggested. He had maintained that the doctrine of self-determination was at the root of all "infidel systems" and that Arminianism when carried to its logical conclusion would result either in deism or in the complete elimination of the notion of sin. Actually the deists were able to dispense with sin without recourse to self-determination. Anthony Collins, for example, was both deist and necessitarian, and Benjamin Franklin united the two streams in his treatise on *Liberty and Necessity.* Also, the deists used arguments to minimize the evil in the universe very much like those of Edwards when he was discussing the perfection of God rather than the imperfection of man.

In reading Edwards we have the opinion that Arminians were heretics—only a few steps removed from deists and as such in the vanguard of liberal theology. Actually some of the Arminians, by denying that grace is irresistible, made salvation harder to obtain than it seemed to be under the Calvinist scheme. Edwards, however, associated Arminianism with a minimal emphasis on grace and a maximal emphasis on human ethics. Essentially Edwards was attacking latitudinarianism rather than the basic theology of Arminius or its English revival as represented by John Wesley and the later *Arminian Magazine.*

The controversy may be visualized through the different perspectives by which Edwards and the Arminians regarded the problem of human behavior. The Arminians, emphasizing morality, considered agency to be the essence of salvation. Edwards, emphasizing the metaphysical concept of God as the prime mover in the universe, considered election to be the essence of salvation. Since Edwards was wont to emphasize metaphysics rather than ethics, we would not expect him to be strong in questions of theoretical morality. He did not remedy this deficiency until he wrote his *Nature of True Virtue.* It should not be necessary to add, however, that crying down good works in his theology had no diminishing effect whatsoever on the high standards of conduct which Edwards practiced in daily living and indeed insisted upon in his sermons and other treatises.

In his treatise on the will, Edwards tackled the problem of moral agency with the aim of proving that virtue and vice, praise and blame, were consistent with necessity rather than with the Arminian notion of liberty. His first point is that even the Arminians admit that God lacks freedom in the sense that his will is necessarily bent to that which is good and holy. At the same time Scripture, custom, and common sense indicate that God is to be praised. The same reasoning applies to Christ. Without going into the question of his conception of the Trinity, Edwards discussed the acts of the will of the human soul of Christ, which were necessarily holy, but which at the same time conformed to the nature of virtue and were worthy of praise. The necessity of Christ's behavior is proved by the promise made by the Father, which made any deviation absolutely impossible.

It was also affirmed in Scripture that the Saviour must be sinless—and here, as in every detail, Scripture had to be fulfilled. No such promises or assurances had surrounded the first Adam—this was the reason why he could fall. That Christ could not fall was not an indication of his being without virtue—a consequence which, Edwards maintained, would be implied in the Arminian system—but proof of his consummate virtue. Since none of Edwards' antagonists would speak out against the virtue of Christ, it might be said that Edwards scored a point at this stage. But, on the other hand, since Christ could easily be considered as belonging to a special category beyond the reach of ordinary mortals, the point could be considered as having little significance.

Edwards' case would seem much stronger had he used in its behalf the other extreme in nature and behavior—the evil angels and fallen man in general. But he would have had a more difficult time proving that we are to blame for the moral necessity of our sin and for our preordained inability to follow the path of virtue. Indeed Edwards does not really handle this problem; he only seems to. He abandons the argument with the assertion that all sin is blamable—no matter how caused and whether necessary or not. When Edwards seems to be reasoning on the question, he is merely pointing out inconsistencies in one of his Arminian foes, Whitby. The latter, quoting St. Augustine's definition of a sin as an action *a quo liberum est abstinere,* had affirmed that one who does evil through necessity is guilty of no fault and worthy of no blame. Edwards answers that, if this be true, all those in Scripture of whom it is said that God "gave them up to their own hearts' lust" should be accounted blameless for continuing in their sins. Judas, in this sense, should be considered blameless, since Christ had given him over and declared his certain damnation.

Apart from this scriptural argument, Edwards contented himself with demonstrating that the Arminian system actually contradicts itself by alleging both self-determination and moral responsibility. If being determined to sin wholly excuses a man, he argues, then a man with a strong bent or inclination to evil is excused to the degree of difficulty which he faces in avoiding it. Thus the degree of blamableness (or moral responsibility) should be reduced in exact inverse proportion to the degree of freedom or self-determination in the will. A strong bent and bias to sin and difficulty in going the other way never can be charged as blamable, according to the Arminian "because as the difficulty is increased, so much the less is required and expected." As far as Edwards is concerned, the Arminian system would logically lead to the complete banishment of guilt and moral responsibility by excusing everyone. It was of course inherent in the doctrine of original sin that all mankind are ridden by sin and none is excused from guilt and moral responsibility, and perhaps Edwards felt that he had no need to demonstrate a doctrine which was clearly affirmed in the Scriptures. In his treatise on original sin, he made his best effort to reconcile blame and necessity, but he still grounded his demonstration on theological rather than ethical arguments.

Edwards found another contradiction in the Arminian contention that guilt for sin is not consistent with necessity in the fact that the Arminians also maintained that fallen man cannot continue in a state of innocence, in other words, that every man will sin at some time or another. This doctrine, according to Edwards, is equivalent to an assertion that sin is consistent with necessity. Quoting from his own sermon "Justification by Faith Alone," Edwards attributed to the

Arminians the view that "God in mercy to mankind has abolished that rigorous constitution or law, that they were under originally; and instead of it, has introduced a more mild constitution, and put us under a new law, which requires no more than imperfect sincere obedience, in compliance with our poor infirm impotent circumstances since the fall." Just what law are these imperfections a breach of?, Edwards demanded. They cannot be infractions of the old law, since this has been abolished. If they are a breach of no law at all, then they cannot be sins, and therefore there was no need for Christ to have died for them. These may be legitimate objections to the Arminian system, but they still do not justify Edwards' position that blame can consist with necessity.

He is not much more satisfactory in the next section of the treatise, that devoted to showing that God's commands and man's obligation to obedience are consistent with moral inability to obey. "Moral inability" describes situations in which men are unable to obey the commands of God, not because of natural impediments, but because of the determination of their will. Edwards again avoids coming to grips with the concept of moral obligation in favor of launching further attacks on the Arminians. He reverts to the notion of self-determination, now arguing that "if there be any sort of act, or exertion of the soul, prior to all free acts of the will or acts of choice in the case, directing and determining what the acts of the will shall be; that act or exertion of the soul can't properly be subject to any command or precept, in any respect whatsoever." This means merely that if there is any force which breaks the chain of cause and effect in human volition, this force exists entirely apart from the will, and the individual cannot be held responsible for it. If the Arminians wish to shift their ground to contingence and argue that "volitions are events that come to pass by pure accident, without any determining cause," this argument also is contrary to the application of laws and precepts. If the will has contingence it is not really subject to commands; if it is biased toward commands it no longer has contingence.

After this demonstration, Edwards abandoned the concept of moral government or justice and contented himself with vindicating moral inability. The mere fact that the will fails to follow divine command obviously implies moral inability in a necessitarian system. Edwards, therefore, felt called upon to answer the objection that the doctrine seems to make all men equally guilty—not in the sense of their all being victims of original sin, which Edwards, of course, accepted, but in the sense of their being "morally unable to will otherwise than they actually do will, in all cases, and equally so, in every instance." In other words, no man is essentially morally better than any other. Edwards replied categorically that all men have the same degree of moral inability—that is, an absolute degree as far as necessity is concerned—but that there are nevertheless moral differences separating men and these moral differences are just as real as physical differences. Even though a man may be unable to resist a vicious action, he may be much further away from performing it habitually than are many other men. In this way he resembles the man who is physically qualified to lift a weight of one hundred pounds and no more. He "is as truly and really unable to lift one hundred and one pounds, as ten thousand pounds; but yet he is further from being able to lift the latter weight than the former." Also a man may succumb to a present evil, but may desire and attempt to discover the means to keep from succumbing to the same evil in the future. In this sense "inability" is a relative term.

To prove that God's commands and precepts are in perfect harmony with man's inability to perform them, Edwards argued that the contrary situation would completely overthrow the Arminian position. If God could command a degree of volition in his creatures no greater than that which they already possessed, there would be no need of commands and precepts; indeed they would be vain and impertinent. In such a system disobedience would be impossible, and for this reason, Edwards argued, the Arminians would not dare to affirm it. Turning the tables against his opponents, however, hardly constituted a vindication of the contrary position, in which obedience is impossible. In his comments on science in his notebooks, Edwards frequently tested his propositions by this method of proving the contrary to be untenable. Yet this is not necessarily proof of the affirmative. We may use the method, for example, to test the assertion that "all women may bear children." The contrary, "no women may bear

[95]

children," is certainly not true—but neither is the original affirmation.

As a corollary to his premise, that acts which men are morally unable to do may properly be the matter of precept or command, Edwards sneaked in a justification of divine invitations and counsels to accept the plan of salvation, on the grounds that these are essentially the same thing as commands. "The main difference between command and invitation" he argued, "consists in the enforcement of the will of him who commands or invites. In the latter it is his *kindness*, the goodness which his will arises from: in the former it is his *authority*." But men are equally incapacitated by moral inability to do what they are directed to do by either command or invitation. This is the ground of the major theological objection to a system combining necessity with original sin and the weightiest problem which Edwards as a preacher had to contend with. How can a minister logically teach that a man's salvation or damnation has been irrevocably ordered from before the creation of the world and still appeal to him to change his way of life in order to accept the Christian plan of salvation? The answer is that the two positions are completely irreconcilable in Edwards' published works, and he never succeeded in bringing them into harmony.

A recent scholar, John H. Gerstner, has painstakingly analyzed all the sermons of Edwards, printed or in manuscript, with this problem in mind and has succeeded in making the sermons consistent with each other. But some of them are, nevertheless, incompatible with the doctrine of necessity. In his role as an evangelist, inspiring and vitalizing the Great Awakening, Edwards spread the message, "Seek and you will find." As a theologian, howeyer, Edwards privately believed, "Seek but you shall not find."

In his preaching Edwards actually taught that salvation is a "free choice" in that nobody is forced to come to Christ. "God has sent me to you to make you the offer," he pleaded. "Christ has sent me to give you an invitation." In his sermons, Edwards affirmed that God never gives salvation unless men seek it first, but as a theologian he believed that salvation comes entirely through God's grace and that no man can seek without a foregoing, igniting spark from God. In his sermons, Edwards leaves one with the impression that all men have the power to seek and that those who do not do so deliberately prefer evil. This is a watering down of the universal moral inability discussed in his treatise. But Edwards' reasoning on the disagreeable points in his sermons is seldom presented in a straightforward manner. I use "disagreeable" to refer to doctrines of exclusiveness (which Edwards concealed or obscured) rather than to those of eternal punishment and the wrath of God, which Edwards consciously used as a means of terrifying his congregation. Gerstner summarizes Edwards' position on seeking salvation as follows: "Being willing to be made willing and being willing are equivalent. So when men begin to seek, they are seeking to be made willing: but they are not willing to be made willing. Indeed, if they were willing to be made willing, they would not need to seek to be made willing; they would be willing before they began to seek." These are words of one or two syllables; even so, we still have difficulty in penetrating to Edwards' real meaning. Imagine the quandary of Edwards' congregations—even considering their familiarity with Scripture and doctrine—as they were forced to cope with the crabbed style and lofty vocabulary of his expositions.

But the confusion vanished when Edwards made his evangelistic appeal. All was clear, simple, and immediate. Despite his rigorous theology, he actually promised in his sermons: "When persons do what they can God usually does for them that which is not in their own power. . . . If men be but sensible of the need of it they ordinarily have it in their power to take likely methods in order to their salvation."

Edwards' method of reconciling the doctrine of election and reprobation with prescribing means for salvation has been rather widely publicized and is considered one of the curiosities of Puritanism. He taught that the individual has absolutely no way of knowing for certain whether he is one of the elect—and that even the most pious and moral person in his behavior may be inevitably destined to damnation. Nevertheless, we should all do everything needful for salvation and hope for the best. By adhering to all the requirements of a Christian life we are at least sure that we have done everything in our power and have committed no act which is sure to keep us from heaven. "A possibility of being saved,"

Edwards told his congregation, "is much to be preferred to a certainty of perishing."

Although this doctrine may make it worth while for a believer in election to lead a moral life and adhere to all the means of salvation within his power, it is nonetheless incompatible with the doctrine of necessity, for it assumes that the individual has within himself the choice of accepting the means or ignoring them. This is the fundamental assumption of any evangelistic appeal. While it may be true that the doctrine of predestination does not preclude evangelism, the doctrine of philosophical necessity, which is far more embracing, would seem to do so.

If one believes that every act is predetermined and foreknown by God, it would seem to follow that there is no use calling upon revival crowds to accept salvation. Edwards never specifically formulated this objection or an answer to it. Had he been pressed, however, he probably would have answered that both the evangelists' appeals and the people's responses are necessary and prearranged by God. He might also have utilized his illustration of God decreeing both the prayers for rain and the rain which followed.

But Edwards also taught in his sermons that only a small number are elected. With this added belief, it would seem even more inconsistent to appeal to large crowds and to assume—as Edwards certainly did—that whole cities or colonies could be saved almost en masse. Also it seems at the very least a type of misrepresentation to accept a theology of election and philosophy of necessity and at the same time to use the concept of free choice as the basis for evangelistic appeals.

In the next section of his treatise on the will Edwards presented a far less compromising conception of morality than in his evangelistic sermons, refuting in great detail the contention of many men that those who sincerely desire and endeavor such spiritual duties as "repentance of sin, love to God, a cordial acceptance of Christ" may be excused if they are incapacitated from attaining to them. Edwards replied scornfully to this soft Arminian morality, stating that it is an absurdity for man to pretend that he should "incline to have an inclination, which at the same time is contrary to his inclination." As an example, Edwards cited the avaricious drunkard who wishes to be cured of his drunkenness but nevertheless persists in it. Such a man may sincerely desire temperance, not because it is a virtue, but only because he wishes to save money. Similarly, a man corrupt and wicked of heart who is carnally inclined may desire out of a fear of eternal torments to have a love for Christ, but his disposition lacks love and gratitude and has no more virtue than a sick man's desire for a "dose he greatly abhors, to save his life." "Being sincere, hearty and in good earnest, is no virtue, unless it be in a thing that is virtuous." Edwards concluded, therefore, prefiguring his later treatise on *True Virtue*, that everything which is not one hundred per cent virtuous is good for nothing—that so-called "sincere endeavours" are really hypocritical. If men do not go the whole way in virtue—being motivated by virtuous intention—there is no value in their moral behavior. Men who "do what they can" in the sense of living up to a moral code to the best of their ability are in Edwards' eyes "not a whit better than if they did nothing at all" unless they act from some virtuous inclination or act of the will. If the motivation is truly virtuous, it arises from holiness in the heart and is a type of necessity.

In his sermons Edwards preached a doctrine much less rigorous—and probably much more likely to produce moral observance in his congregation. One may seek salvation for a selfish motive, Edwards announced from the pulpit, and even though such a motivation is not morally good, it is justified. In the same way, the performing of good works for selfish ends is evil, but is less evil than not doing them at all. In keeping with his doctrine of a hierarchy of rewards in heaven and punishments in hell, Edwards also preached that, "if you will live a moral life you will surely have a less punishment." It is hard to reconcile this with the type of black-or-white, yes-or-no salvation implied by the doctrine of imputed righteousness.

In his treatise, moreover, Edwards did not shrink even from asserting that there is no reason to think that God will make any provision to afford salvation to the heathen because of their endeavors, no matter how sincere, "to find out the will of the deity, and to please him, according to their light." This is a position on which Christians found themselves vulnerable to the attack of the deists, who argued that a just

God would not single out for favor a special race or chosen people but would make any religious privileges equally available to all mankind. Most orthodox Christians of all sects uneasily affirmed that God made some sort of special dispensation for those heathen who had no opportunity of hearing the Christian message as well as for all those born before the time of Christ, but Edwards adhered to his rigorous doctrine of exclusion, not even promising the virtuous heathens a favored room in hell. He held to this position even though later in the treatise he described the Stoics as "the greatest, wisest and most virtuous of all the heathen philosophers; and in their doctrine and practice [those who] came the nearest to Christianity." Edwards also privately held the theory, which we shall return to later, that the high religious notions of the heathen philosophers were not a result of mere natural reason, but a manifestation of God's revelation to such men as Abraham and Noah. Edwards' rigor was a product of the need he felt for justifying the wrath of God as an essential part of the justice of God.

Chapter 6

SOME ETHICAL PROBLEMS

For Edwards, "What must I do to be saved?" remained the most important question in human experience, and, as an evangelist, he felt that the answer was clear and simple. In his treatise, however, he opened the way to discussion of a related question, "What must be my motivation to be saved?", and he recognized that the answer was entangled in abstruse and perplexing propositions. His discussion of the criteria for salvation touches upon two of the ethical questions most widely debated in nontheological terms in the eighteenth century, although Edwards' emphasis upon doctrine effectively conceals the pragmatic ethical implications of his thought.

These questions were introduced by the Earl of Shaftesbury in his *Inquiry concerning Virtue* as difficulties consequent to his principle that both reason and affection are requisite to virtue. According to his definition, virtue consists in the affections being directed toward that which reason teaches is good. The fundamental test of the virtue of an act, therefore, is its intention, not—as the utilitarians maintained—its results. It is not an action that causes harm which is iniquitous, wicked, and wrong, according to Shaftesbury, but anything that is done through unequal or unbalanced affection. Sometimes a virtuous action may actually have harmful results or a vicious action be salutary in its results. As an illustration of the former, Shaftesbury cites the example of a dutiful son aiming at an enemy and by mistake or ill chance happening to kill his father. This action would not be evil. Wrong exists only in acts caused by insufficient or misguided affection: for example, a son showing no concern for the safety of his father or passing over his father to give succor to an indifferent person.

Edwards is no more systematic than Shaftesbury in assigning the relative portions of reason and affection in virtue, but he agrees completely that intention is its essence. We have seen that he accords no virtue to the drunkard who wishes to curb his vicious inclination merely in order to save money. In his miscellanies, moreover, Edwards gives an example much better adapted to the theories of Shaftesbury. It is still "an old notorious drunkard," but one this time uncomplicated by a mercenary spirit. If this plain drunkard be under a command to forsake his drunkenness, being required to do so under pain of eternal damnation; and if he have some kind of willingness to forsake it—i.e., if his reason tells him that the pain of eternal damnation will countervail all his pleasure from drinking—but if his actual forsaking it has no connection with an act of will (the abstinence being caused by imprisonment or other external circumstance), he is not excused from the penalties of the command—or, in Shaftesbury's terms, his behavior is not virtuous.

Edwards presented an even more lurid illustration in his miscellanies, one which did not pass over into his treatise in any form. A man with a "most amiable and agreeable and every way deserving woman for his wife," whom he is required to love and choose above all women, is nevertheless "overpowered by a violent lust for some vile and notorious strumpet." He realizes that his lust will prove the ruin of himself and his family and he "wishes that he loved his wife as he does his harlot." But "this indirect willingness to cleave to his wife in his love and choice does not at all excuse him for the want of actual love and choice."

The second difficulty which Shaftesbury underscored concerns the struggle against temptation as an element in virtue. According to one classic point of view, there can be no virtue without a strong measure of self-denial, of going contrary to one's basic inclinations. As Shaftesbury expressed it: "If by temper any one is passionate, angry, fearful, amorous; yet resists these passions, and notwithstanding the force of their impression, adheres to virtue, we say commonly in this case that the virtue is the greater." We applaud the virtue of such a person more than we should naturally do if he were free of his temptation and evil propensities. But this is not equivalent to saying, Shaftesbury insists, that the person who resists vicious inclinations is more virtuous than the one who has no contrary impulses and follows virtue out of his natural affections and inclination. The man with evil inclinations, who abandons these inclinations to become motivated entirely by virtuous affections, is simply more virtuous after his change than before. Shaftesbury failed to convince all his contemporaries, arousing the particular derision of Bernard Mandeville, who affirmed that all the ancients had taught that there can be no virtue without self-denial and charged that Shaftesbury was the first to believe the contrary. According to Mandeville's sardonic view, Shaftesbury "seems to require and expect Goodness in his Species, as we do a sweet Taste in Grapes and China Oranges."

In America, Benjamin Franklin carried on the debate by printing a discourse in the *Pennsylvania Gazette*, categorically affirming: *"That* SELF-DENIAL *is not* the ESSENCE *of* VIRTUE." Franklin extended the subject far beyond the treatment Shaftesbury had given it and brought to the controversy the concepts of merit and reward which were fundamental to Edwards. The greatest degree of merit, Franklin insisted, belongs to the man unhindered by temptations to vice, and to him also belongs praise or reward. It would be ridiculous to assume that a patriot is less deserving of praise because his public spirit is natural or to affirm that a man who performs a service out of benevolent inclination deserves less praise than another who performs the same act against his inclination. "The Truth is," Franklin concluded, "that Temperance, Justice, Charity, &c. are Virtues, whether practis'd with or against our Inclinations; and the Man who practises them, merits our Love and Esteem: And Self-denial is neither good nor bad, but as 'tis apply'd: He that denies a vicious Inclination is Virtuous in proportion to his Resolution, but the most perfect Virtue is above all Temptation, such as the Virtue of the Saints in Heaven."

This is exactly the reasoning of Edwards when he maintains in his treatise that the moral excellence of God and Christ is necessary, yet truly virtuous and praiseworthy, and that the virtuous behavior of Christ is worthy of rewards. In his miscellanies, moreover, Edwards discussed the problem in relation to human beings as he ridiculed the notion that determined acts are not blameworthy. Like Franklin, he affirmed that it is utterly preposterous to assume that "if any person be naturally of an excellent spirit, a disposition strongly inclining him to virtue and the most amiable actions, so far does it take from the commendableness and praise-worthiness of his actions." And it would be an equally ludi-crous way of thinking, Edwards argued, to assume that "if a man be naturally a very ill-natured man, and from that ill nature does often treat his neighbors maliciously and with great indignity, his neighbors ought to excuse and not to be angry with him so far as what he does is from ill nature.

In no place does Edwards have very much to say about the internal struggle of the man with vicious inclinations who succeeds in dominating them out of a love of virtue, although he specifically labeled self-denial a moral command of God in his *Thoughts concerning . . . Revival.* In a sense this praise of mastery over one's self cannot be reconciled with his theory in the treatise on the will of the prevalence of the strongest motive. In citing Christ as an example of pure holiness who represents the highest virtue and whose conduct deserves the highest praise, Edwards overlooked the dramatic scene of Christ's temptation by Satan and subsequent victory. He was thus able to avoid an explanation of how the interpreta-tion of the episode as a heroic struggle against temptation could be made to conform with God's foreknowledge that Christ would be victorious.

As Shaftesbury and Franklin interpreted it, the doctrine that deeds are to be accounted virtuous in proportion to the degree of virtue which motivates them, has nothing to do with the system of necessity; but the concept of internal in-clinations is inherently related to Edwards' entire theological scheme, involving necessity, original sin, and efficacious grace. Going back to Adam, the Arminians had maintained that the father of mankind could not have been originally righteous, since righteousness depends upon a choice. Adam was righteous only after he had chosen to be righteous. Edwards answered that he must have been righteous at the start, for virtue as a "positive" thing must take rise from something. It cannot come after a choice and be the result of it. "If the first virtuous act of will or choice be from a preceding act of will or choice, that preceding act of choice must be a virtuous act of choice, which is contrary to the supposition. For then there would be a preceding act of choice before the first virtuous act of choice." Virtue can proceed, therefore, from nothing but God's immediate influence. It follows then that all choices depend upon the degree of virtue infused into every being by God.

Edwards also uses the principle of motivated virtue to attack the Arminian notion of indifference. If, as the Arminians maintained, a virtuous act must be performed in a state of liberty and indifference, it will follow that, "in order to the virtuousness of an act, the heart must be indifferent . . . and the more indifferent and cold the heart is with relation to the act which is performed, so much the better." Is this concept, Edwards asked, agreeable in the light of nature or "to the notions which mankind, in all ages, have of virtue, that it lies in that which is contrary to indifference, even in the tendency and inclination of the heart to virtuous action; and that the stronger the inclination . . . the more virtuous the *heart,* and so much the more praiseworthy the *act* which proceeds from it?" It is odd that Edwards should so confidently characterize as universally accepted a principle which was still highly debatable in his own time. We remember that Mandeville had charged Shaftesbury with being the first to reject the view that self-denial was essential to virtue.

In his rebuttal of the Arminian position, Edwards used his standard attack upon indifference. If the virtuous act is determined by a preceding choice, then the quality of indifference does not exist; and if it is not determined by an act of choice it cannot be virtuous, according to Arminian principles, because the will is not self-determined in it. This is really a proof that self-determination and indifference cannot exist at the same time—a very strong argument which Edwards had not enunciated as such in the part of his treatise devoted to demolishing the Arminian notion of freedom. He carries more conviction in the ethical phase of the debate by means of his examples. If one were to see one's neighbor or friend in extreme distress which could easily be alleviated, "the being indifferent, for a moment, would be highly vicious and vile." The same would be true if one were faced with a proposal to blaspheme God or to murder a parent.

Another disadvantage of the theory of indifference is that

it cannot ascribe viciousness or virtue to habits or dispositions of the heart, "which are contrary to indifference, and imply in their nature the very destruction and exclusion of it." Also, if indifference is necessary to moral agency, such results of evil disposition of heart or habitual depravity of inclination as covetousness, pride, malice, or cruelty are the more excusable the more they are products of habit. "And, on the contrary, whatever excellent disposition and inclinations they have, so much are they the less virtuous." Such a supposition, Edwards charges, will effectively exclude virtue and vice from the world, for practically all human behavior is a result of "propensity, disposition or habit."

This is one of the few sections in his philosophical works in which Edwards appears as a pragmatic moralist, insisting on the reality of virtue and vice in the everyday world. When writing about original sin, Edwards usually assumes that no human behavior can be considered virtuous or merit praise, but when answering the Arminians Edwards asserts that virtuous behavior exists and that it counts for God's approval. From the perspective of original sin, everything is all black or all white; but from the perspective of practical morality there are seen to be degrees of virtue and vice. In refutation of Arminian indifference, on the grounds that it banished virtue and vice (while overlooking the fact that his own rigorous conception of original sin has the same effect), Edwards printed a long list of virtuous deeds and inclinations that he assumed to be morally praiseworthy, including "universal benevolence to mankind."

Edwards gave his final blow to the notion of freedom in moral agency by asserting that it could no more be reconciled with motivation in moral action than with the development of habits and dispositions. If it be true that the soul chooses without any motive—as the Arminians allege—then its acts would have no end or intention and therefore no more virtue "than in the motion of the smoke, which is driven to and fro by the wind." By this reasoning Edwards tried to turn the tables against the Arminians, who had contended that Calvinistic necessity was inconsistent with the use of counsels, exhortations, invitations and expostulations. He insisted that the same inconsistency exists with the Arminian notion of self-determinism, which would deny virtue to any motivated action, including a response to a command; that therefore it would invalidate all the means God has "used with men, in ordinance, or providence." Therefore that "horrid blasphemous consequence will certainly follow from the Arminian doctrine, which they charge on others; namely, that God acts an inconsistent part in using so many counsels, warnings, invitations, entreaties, etc. with sinners, to induce 'em to forsake sin . . . and that all are insincere and fallacious."

This is the point at which Edwards makes the two systems conflict most sharply, for he judges them by a criterion inherent in both: that God attempts to persuade men and holds them responsible for their behavior. Here also the weaknesses of both systems are apparent—the Arminian in metaphysics, the Calvinist in pragmatic morality. But metaphysical considerations seem less significant if one accepts Dr. Johnson's contention that all argument is for necessity, all experience against.

Having denied the possibility of the very existence of self-determinism, Edwards proceeded to condemn it on the grounds that even if it could exist, it would be incompatible with any system of ethical judgment, for it would destroy the continuity of individual behavior. In a sense, there would be no personal moral identity. The Arminians certainly did not deny the concept of strongest motive, but argued that the decision is sometimes not simple or automatic as the necessitarian position implied. It is possible, they felt, to make a conscious attempt to place salutary motives against vicious ones—benevolent against narrowly selfish. The mind may be able to dwell upon one set of motives rather than another and, in so doing, carry out a type of self-denial.

Chapter 7

DETERMINISM DEFENDED

Most significant, in the last part of Edwards' treatise, is his defense of his system against three of the primary objections raised against it: (1) that it makes man a mere machine, (2) that it presents God in the same guise, and (3) that it makes God the author of sin.

(1) Edwards' ringing argument that man is not a machine has been quoted by nearly every one of his disciples. It illustrates Edwards' clever use of words in making them seem to mean almost the contrary of their ordinary signification. This semantic sophistry, which Edwards elsewhere accused the Arminians of using, is revealed below by the qualifying additions in brackets, which Edwards himself failed to supply.

Man is entirely, perfectly and unspeakably different from a mere machine, in that he has reason and understanding, and has a faculty of will, and so is capable of volition and choice [but that choice is limited to the strongest motive which is inevitably fixed by a chain of cause and effect from the beginning of things]; and in that, his will is guided by the dictates or views of his understanding; and in that his external actions and behavior, and in many respects also his thoughts, and the exercises of his mind, are subject to his will; so that he has liberty to act [but not to will] according to his choice, and do [but not will] what he pleases [but what he pleases is limited to the strongest motive]; and by means of these things, is capable of moral habits and moral acts, such inclinations and actions as according to the common sense of mankind, are worthy of praise, esteem, love and reward; or on the contrary, of disesteem, detestation, indignation and punishment.

Actually Edwards' position would be stronger if he were to admit that man is very much like a machine—a concept which Franklin did not shrink from in his dissertation on liberty and necessity. Ridiculing the notion of free will or power to do or refrain from doing, Franklin observed that the existence of such a power would devastate the moral system: "It is as if an ingenious Artificer, having fram'd a curious Machine or Clock, and put its many intricate Wheels and Powers in such a Dependance on one another, that the whole might move in the most exact Order and Regularity, had nevertheless plac'd in it several other Wheels endu'd with an independent *Self-Motion*, but ignorant of the general Interest of the Clock; and these would every now and then be moving wrong, disordering the true Movement, and making continual Work for the Mender: which might better be prevented, by depriving them of that Power of Self-Motion, and placing them in a Dependance on the regular Part of the Clock." Edwards was afraid to draw such a comprehensive parallel, even though it fits his scheme as precisely as Franklin's. He first of all categorically denied the machine comparison, and then as a corollary attempted to salvage it in part. "Machines are guided by an understanding cause, by the skillful hand of the workman or owner," he affirmed as a second thought; "whereas the will of man under the Arminian scheme" is left to the guidance of nothing but absolute blind contingence.

This blind contingence, Edwards continued, is less compatible with the use of means and endeavors for the avoiding of sin than is the system of necessity. For endeavors to be valid, he argued, there must be a fixed connection between those events to which the qualities of virtue and vice are attached and the endeavors which we use to attain those qualities, and this connection is implied in the necessitarian scheme. But in a scheme based on blind contingence, there can be no cause-and-effect relationship.

As we have already seen, Edwards explained the relation between means and their results as belonging to the general chain of events in the world. The means we use to avoid sin or follow virtue are as much established as anything else is. If we pray for relief from wickedness, we do so as part of the chain of cause and effect. We are literally obliged to pray. This concept is greatly amplified in Edwards' miscellanies, where he explains the harmony and order based on the perfect relationship between God's decrees. "Thus, God decrees rain in drought because He decrees the earnest prayers of His people, or thus, He decrees the prayers of His people because He decrees rain." The first is not necessarily a condition of the second any more than the second is a condition of the first —they are merely harmoniously established and foredetermined. "Thus also, when He decrees diligence and industry, He decrees riches and prosperity; when He decrees prudence, He often decrees success; when He decrees striving, then often He decrees the obtaining of the Kingdom of Heaven [notice the prudent *often* in the last two examples]; when He decrees the preaching of the Gospel, then He decrees the bringing home of souls to Christ."

Elsewhere in his miscellanies, Edwards explains why we should not object to "praying and striving and attending on meeting if all was irreversibly determined by God before." According to his explanation: "Decrees of our everlasting state were not before our prayers and strivings, for these are as much present with God from all eternity as they are the moment they are present with us; they are present or not as He decrees, or rather are the same, and they did as really exist in eternity with respect to God as much at one time as another. Therefore, we can no more further argue that these will be in vain because God has foredetermined than we can that they would be in vain if they existed as law or the decree; for so they do, inasmuch as they are a part of it." Edwards really evades the problem here by looking upon God as beyond time and considering mortals as within it. Essentially he says nothing more than that both the prayers and the subsequent events are decreed. Of course, according to Edwards' idealism, all creation is nothing but an idea of God; it follows, therefore, that all things from eternity are equally present with God, he has no succession, and "there is no alteration made in idea by presence and absence, as there is in us." But the question at issue is not whether there is a succession for God, but whether there is for ordinary mortals.

It is odd that Edwards did not fall back on the interpretation of the role of prayer that he had offered in his *Treatise concerning Religious Affections*. Here he had unequivocally asserted that the function of prayer is not to inform God of his greatness nor to ask him to fulfill our own desires. These things God already knows and has considered. Instead prayer is intended "suitably to affect our hearts with the things we express."

In a sermon Edwards once asked the question—related to his controversy over the sacrament—whether the body of men who are not committed to God are not hypocrites whenever they pray. He answered that although prayer is a universal duty, no merely natural man is capable of performing it in the proper fashion. But even insincere prayer is better than none at all since it enables the sinner to avoid a more willful act of disobedience. It is better, Edwards argues, to "pray out of self-love than neglect prayer out of self-love." Such prayer is "materially evil but formally good." In other words, prayer has practical benefit even though it may in itself do nothing to procure one's salvation.

In his treatise on the will, Edwards had affirmed that the connection of the succession or train of antecedents and consequents from the very beginning of things was either based on the established laws of nature or caused by "sovereign immediate interpositions of divine power." On the surface, there would seem to be an incompatibility between the laws of nature and divine interposition, in the sense that the latter would upset the former—or at least interfere with the unbroken chain of events upon which God's foreknowledge is predicated—unless it be assumed that God's foredeterminism included every interposition contrary to the laws of nature. Presumably this is the assumption Edwards made. At least, in his miscellanies, he indicated that God in arranging the motion, rest and direction of every atom in the physical universe had to make "a nice allowance . . . for the miracles which should be needful." Edwards also indicated that "God who does this must necessarily be omniscient and know every least thing that must happen through eternity." Probably he would also say that when God intervened to change human actions, he had also predetermined his interpositions and made allowances for them.

[111]

Although Edwards was more concerned with the metaphysical than the ethical side of theology, he was usually careful to point out the practical value of the doctrines he advocated—or in eighteenth-century language, how the doctrines could be "improved." There was only one objection to the doctrine of necessity based on moral behavior that Edwards would admit had any validity. This was the supposition that people might assume that since everything was foreordained, it would be folly for them to endeavor means for their salvation and therefore it would be entirely justifiable for them to "take their ease." But Edwards argued that deciding that one can do nothing about one's salvation and therefore giving up all attempts at virtue is in itself making a choice. To neglect voluntarily the means for one's own salvation is inconsistent with the principles one would be pretending to act upon. This is all that Edwards says on the point. He fails to affirm or deny that one can actually make such a choice, probably recognizing that to affirm it would amount to repudiating his entire necessitarian argument. Yet his counsel in evangelistic sermons—that believers should act as though they were among the elect in order not to commit a sin that in itself would nullify their chances for salvation—certainly implies that a choice is possible. And this counsel is equally inconsistent with the principles it is established upon. The system of necessity allows for neither the aspiring saint to choose a life of virtuous endeavor nor the despairing sinner to choose a life of ease. Yet Edwards "improved" the doctrine by supporting the first and rejecting the second.

In justice to Edwards, we must recognize that he was following a respectable tradition. As Pierre Bayle had remarked about the Stoics, their principles of an absolutely inevitable fatalism should have led them never to be concerned about anything whatsoever and never to use exhortations, menaces, censures or promises: "However there were never philosophers who more widely used all these things than they, and all their conduct made apparent that they believed themselves to be entirely the masters of their destiny."

In Edwards' personal life, as we have seen, his faith in God wavered when he knew in advance that the outcome of an event would be adverse.

(2) One of Edwards' points used to prove that liberty is not essential to moral agency had been the example of God as a being of perfect virtue who lacks liberty. But he recognized that to some people the contention that God's will, like man's, is necessary in its determinations, would seem, as Watts expressed it, to turn God into "a kind of mechanical medium of fate." Edwards retorted that "This is declaiming, rather than arguing; and an application to men's imaginations and prejudices, rather than to mere reason." But he nevertheless answered the charge that his doctrine turned God into a machine, a charge that appears serious because it is based on the assumptions that there is a privilege or dignity associated with being without moral necessity, and that there is disadvantage or dishonor associated with being subject to it. But these assumptions are invalid, Edwards contended, for moral necessity "argues no imperfection, inferiority or dependence, nor any want of dignity, privilege or ascendancy." Certainly God is not in any sense disparaged by the recognition that God's will is determined by supreme wisdom and supreme holiness.

·In this discussion of the powers and nature of God, Edwards soared to the uppermost reaches of abstract metaphysical speculation, which in theory he deplored and apologized for. Yet we sense that this is the realm that he found most congenial and from which he obtained his greatest satisfaction.

In all things where there is a real element of preference, Edwards continued, there is no dishonor in God's operating from necessity. In all things that God does, he always chooses that that is preferable according to superior fitness. For Edwards, God is in this sense absolutely and completely under necessity: there are no instances whatsoever of indifference toward or equality in fitness in God's acts. Edwards' opponents usually used two arguments to prove that God could act with indifference: first, that some objects of choice revealed absolutely no difference, one from the other; and, second, that some objects of choice had such insignificant differences that God's decision one way or the other would be of no consequence. In favor of the first supposition, it had been alleged that since the various parts of infinite time and space are perfectly alike, God could have created our world at another time rather than when he did. Edwards answered with the Kant-like argument that our imagination cannot conceive of either infinite space or time or distinct parts or stages in relationship to the deity. " 'Tis equally improper, to talk of months and years of the divine existence, and mile-squares of deity." Since we cannot ascribe our notions of time to God, any arguments based upon them are invalid. The second argument, an attempt to prove that God could operate in an area of indifference, concerned the placing of identical atoms in various parts of the world: for example, those in water or in the fiery particles of the sun. According to this argument, a drop of water in one ocean could just as well exist anywhere else in the rivers and oceans of the world. Edwards answered that since we must suppose matter to be infinitely divisible, it is unlikely that any two particles should be exactly alike. And even if two identical particles existed, one would fit in a certain place better than the other—and each would be serving a different end where it was placed. Edwards furthered his argument by analogy: God often spoke to Moses, the identical words, *I am Jehovah,* but each utterance served a different end.

Edwards came very close to reaffirming the reasoning of Leibniz that this is the best of all possible worlds. The advocates of indifference had alleged that "innumerable things which are determined by the divine will, and chosen and done by God rather than others, differ from those that are not chosen" in so insignificant or inconsiderable a manner that it would be unreasonable to suppose that the ultimate determination has anything to do with any superior fitness or goodness of things. Edwards answered that it "would be unreasonable to suppose, that God made one atom in vain, or without any end or motive." The smallest atom in the universe requires as much of God's power as does Jupiter to uphold it.

In a theology that distinguishes between saints and sinners, promising salvation to the one and threatening damnation to the other, the rationale of God's choice becomes a serious matter, transcending the importance of his placing of atoms or even planets. When God, through his grace, decides between the elect and the reject, is God entirely free in his decision or is he subject to necessity? The Arminians argued that the supposition of necessity derogates from God's goodness and from the obligation of the saved to thankfulness for their benefits. Edwards answered that it derogates no more from God's goodness to suppose that his benevolence is based on wisdom than to suppose that it is based on chance. Neither Edwards nor the Arminians would maintain that God's motive in bestowing his favors would depend on any moral quality in the object, since such a relationship would reduce the "manifestation of the freeness and sovereignty of his grace." But Edwards contended that it might still be within the framework of creating the perfect universe for God to distinguish such a person. In other words, God's grace would not be the reward of the person's merit, but the expression of natural fitness in God's wise design.

As Edwards pursued the inquiry into God's grace, he deliberately refrained from stating all his thoughts on the subject. One wonders whether he was afraid of the consequences. Instead of affirmatively stating his own beliefs and conclusions, he limited himself to rhetorical questions and affirmations of generally received truths. None will deny, he reasoned, that in some instances, God acts from wise design in determining the particular subjects of his favors. Then Edwards inquired "whether in these instances God's goodness is less manifested, than in those wherein God has no aim or end at all." Edwards does not admit in so many words that God may act arbitrarily with no wise end in view—but he carefully keeps from denying it. Indeed he implies his assent to the proposition by asking: "How shall it be known when God is influenced by some wise aim, and when not?" As an example of a wise aim, Edwards cited the conversion of Paul, who had been a persecutor of Christians. Edwards says no more on the subject, but it is obvious that God did not reward Paul for his virtue—in Edwards' terminology, there was no "Covenant of Work." Instead God followed his arbitrary will—which was, nevertheless, according to Edwards, under moral necessity.

As we have seen, a rigid system wherein only the virtuous receive rewards would place God under the terms of a contract and thereby reduce his omnipotence. Against this system, Edwards specifically maintained that God may choose to bestow his favors on a vicious rather than a virtuous person. He "may choose this object rather than another, as having a superior fitness to answer the ends, designs and inclinations of his goodness; being more sinful, and so more miserable and necessitous than others; the inclinations of infinite mercy and benevolence may be more gratified." This amounts to the admission that there is no principle of equality in the bestowal of God's favors even though they may be designed for the general good.

In backing away from the Arminian emphasis on morality, Edwards seems to have made too great a concession. Had he been called upon for comment, Edwards might have replied that God's rectitude is absolute (in the sense that all creatures are deficient and deserve to be damned), but that his benevolence is a matter of choice or discrimination. This explanation, based on Edwards' theory of original sin, salvages God's justice in a general sense, but does nothing to vindicate those inequities that seem the inevitable consequence of stressing God's arbitrary will.

(3) If one accepts the doctrine of original sin—or for that matter the teaching of experience that the world abounds in evil—and at the same time believes that man has no freedom of will, it might seem that man is not responsible for his evil deeds. In this sense, God is made the author of sin. Edwards, in attempting to deny that his system puts God into this light, followed the forensic method he had used in virtually every preceding step—that of transferring the accusation. He argued that the Arminian system teaches the same doctrine; first, in admitting that God withheld his assistance in helping man avoid evil from devils and damned spirits and, second, in affirming God's foreknowledge of every sin that was ever committed. Then, appealing for a clarification of terms, Edwards explained that he would not admit that God could be "the author of sin" if this means "the *doer* of a wicked thing," but he would accept the phrase if it means that God may sometimes not hinder sin while he is disposing of events for excellent ends. In this sense Edwards declared that "it was the design of God, that Christ should be *crucified*, and that for this end he came into the world." Immediately afterwards, Edwards reduced the universal force of his concession by affirming as a general rule that "God sometimes permits sin to be committed." Sin in the world is like frost, which is caused by the withdrawal of sun, not *by* the sun. Thus "sin is not the fruit of any positive

agency or influence of the most High, but on the contrary, arises from the withholding of his action and energy." As an analogy this seems plausible, but in a broader sense it amounts to the admission that men are under necessity when led in a good direction, but at liberty when they sin. To be sure, Edwards adds that men commit sin "only when God leaves 'em *to themselves*" and then they do so necessarily. But this seems to indicate they are under a twofold necessity when they are good, a single necessity when they are bad.

Edwards next maintained that it is better that good and evil should be ordered and disposed than that they be the result of chance. Thus agents may be ordered to do something for evil ends which may have good results, for example, Joseph's brothers selling him into slavery. Similarly, from the human point of view, the crucifixion was the most heinous act committed in history, but from the divine view it was the most glorious. Since we cannot maintain that it would be better for the world not to have moral evil, we cannot argue that providence is anything but wise and holy.

Edwards anticipated that the objection would be raised that this scheme amounts to asserting "that God may do evil that good may come," which is an immoral doctrine. Edwards argued that there is no moral evil at all involved in God's dispensation since evil requires either that a thing be unfit and unsuitable in its own nature, that it have a bad tendency, or that it proceed from an evil disposition. None of these conditions can be attributed to God's ordering immoral acts for good ends. The immoral action of a human being may have all of these ingredients, but God's ordering it has none. To many people this may seem to be an evasion, as does Edwards' similar explanation in his miscellanies that God may determine sinful actions without determining sin: that he does not "decree the actions that are sinful as sin, but decrees them as joined" to sin. "God decrees that they shall be sinful for the sake of the good that He causes to arise from the sinfulness of the acts, whereas man decrees them for the sake of the evil that it intends." This is in line with his explanation of causation as exemplified by prayers for rain and the rain itself—one event may be connected with an event which precedes it, but not necessarily growing out of it or inherently related to it.

Edwards used this departmentalizing process to explain how sin entered the world. God allowed or permitted sin, but he did not cause it. It arose from man's imperfections which led to his first evil act, and it was in no sense the product of God's appointment. Edwards undoubtedly already had in mind his later treatise on original sin, for he added that the difficulties surrounding the subject "would require room that can't be here allowed." But he added his usual justification that the Arminian system is subject to the same difficulties.

In his conclusion, Edwards anticipated the refutations or attacks of his opponents and impugned them in advance. After predicting with a large measure of insight that his whole performance would be "treated with triumph and insult," Edwards ran through the major Calvinistic doctrines which he felt had been supported and defended by his proofs of necessity. In regard to the doctrine of the total depravity and corruption of man's nature, he had demonstrated that the only necessity to sinning is a moral necessity, which does not excuse sin and does not nullify commands and exhortations. He had also vindicated the doctrine of efficacious and irresistible grace; the view that a sinner's conversion is wrought entirely by God's influence—again, through moral necessity. Edwards specifically declared that when a man sins, he does so through God's permission, but when a man is virtuous, his virtue comes through God's positive influence. He did not seem to feel that this double standard represents God as unjust, unfair, or capricious. Edwards' system had also vindicated the doctrine of absolute, eternal personal election of the saints, for it follows from the divinely inspired system of cause and effect that God "makes some saints, and not others, on design or purpose." Edwards added that "however Christ may be said to *die for all*," yet "God has the actual salvation or redemption of a certain number in his proper absolute design, and of a certain number only." Even though Edwards could insist that God may be just and within his rights to condemn all mankind for sin, the system of selection seems unfair because of the moral disproportion between God and men. Edwards presents God as judging men according to his own high standards, finding all guilty and then saving a small number. But we may ask: Why has God singled out some and not others? Chance, con-

[118]

tingence, whim—all the notions that Edwards condemns in the Arminian scheme—would seem to be involved in God's choice. Finally, Edwards' necessitarianism vindicated the doctrine of the infallible and necessary perseverance of the saints, which the Arminians had objected to on the grounds that it does not require perseverance in virtue and holiness. There is perseverance in the necessitarian system, but it is based on the infallible certainty of events rather than continued exercise of a self-determining power.

Edwards confidently affirmed that all these doctrines follow from his proof of necessity, and commentators have almost universally followed him in admitting the soundness of his chain of logic. If they disagree with any of the subsumed doctrines, they are likely to base their disagreement on the grounds that the necessitarian scheme itself is faulty. Actually these doctrines are not at all inevitable consequences of necessitarianism; they only seem to be because of Edwards' skillful use of the necessitarian position to beat down the Arminian opposition. Many people will accept Edwards' proofs for necessity—including the distinction between natural and moral—who will not accept the other Calvinistic doctrines. Among other eighteenth-century philosophers we might mention Godwin and Priestley.

In the last paragraph of his treatise Edwards lashed out at the writers who had not scrupled to say that if the Calvinistic doctrines are true "then God is unjust and cruel, and guilty of manifest deceit and double-dealing," and others who had asserted that "if any book which pretends to be Scripture, teaches such doctrines, that alone is sufficient warrant for mankind to reject it." Edwards, because of his sparing recourse to Scripture citation, cannot really be said to have proved that the Calvinistic doctrines are scriptural. But because he and many Arminians assumed that these doctrines depended on the truth or falsity of the necessitarian argument, his success in defending necessity seemed equally to bolster the rest of Calvinism. For this reason, his treatise worked to strengthen the faith of those who were already strong Calvinists and to undermine the Christianity of those who were not.

Chapter 8

ORIGINAL SIN

If Edwards' treatise on the will has little reference to Scripture, his treatise on original sin, *The Great Christian Doctrine of Original Sin Defended,* 1758, consists of little else but citation and interpretation of Bible verses. Although there are important philosophical issues involved in the subject of original sin, Edwards relegated them to the background in his zeal to discredit his antagonist John Taylor, a liberal English dissenter who had published a searching examination of the doctrine, charging it with being highly injurious to the character of God, of pouring contempt upon human nature, and of promoting melancholy, ill-nature and mutual hatred. Even more shocking and dangerous to fundamentalists such as Edwards, Taylor had charged that the doctrine did not exist in the Bible at all. The whole system of placing the destiny of mankind upon the shoulders of Adam, Taylor maintained, had grown out of fiction and chimera, and Scripture had been engrafted in it with neither truth nor relevance.

The basic philosophical question underlying the discussion is whether the original nature of man is good or evil, benevolent or selfish, and it had been treated acutely and wittily by Shaftesbury and Hutcheson on one side, Hobbes and Mandeville on the other. Edwards ignored the broader aspects of the problem—the evidence of observation in the areas of psychology, sociology and economics—and confined himself almost exclusively to proving against Taylor that original sin was indeed taught by Scripture. He was far more anxious to demolish Taylor than to penetrate to the truth concerning human nature.

Edwards faced no great difficulty in gaining this narrow objective, for literal interpretation of the Bible certainly upholds original sin. Taylor was trying to defend a benevolent system of Christianity, latitudinarian like that of the Cambridge Platonists, while still adhering to the fundamental assumption that the literal meaning of the Scriptures must always be accepted. Since it was impossible to reconcile the two approaches, Edwards had no trouble exposing Taylor's inconsistencies and making him seem ridiculous. Systems like Taylor's, embodying concepts of benevolent morality, could be made compatible with Christianity only after fundamentalism gave way a century or so later to higher criticism, allegorical interpretation and doctrinal renovation.

Taylor's revolt against the doctrine of original sin, a doctrine which seemed to portray human nature in the blackest colors and make out God to be vindictive and vengeful, grew out of the application to theology of the benevolent philosophy of Shaftesbury and Hutcheson. Shaftesbury himself had previously charged Calvinistic divines with promoting the selfish system of Thomas Hobbes by their disparaging portrayals of human nature. Rejecting evil and depravity, Shaftesbury and Hutcheson taught that the universe is controlled by a mild and benevolent God and that man is governed by an inherent moral sense, disposing him toward the good and the beautiful.

Shaftesbury, a deist, was not recognized in public by most English and American clergymen, but Hutcheson, a theologically trained Professor of Moral Philosophy at Glasgow, was generally esteemed by dissenters and seldom accused of heterodoxy. Since Taylor's and Hutcheson's theological systems had many points in common, Taylor quoted Hutcheson extensively and acknowledged his discipleship. Edwards was drawn subconsciously to Hutcheson's systematic portrayal of divine order and beauty, but was prevented by his Calvinism from any open espousal of a benevolent system. Quoting, for example, one of Taylor's favorite passages from Hutcheson, one which Taylor had used in the attack on original sin, Edwards carefully refrained from any disparaging remarks about Hutcheson or his system. More than this, Edwards conformed with the opinion of Shaftesbury and Hutcheson on a fundamental point which he had already much insisted upon in his treatise on the will—that good actions come from a good disposition. Edwards again used this argument in upholding original sin and quoted Hutcheson approvingly to support the contention that Adam had a virtuous disposition before his fall. He denied, however, what both Hutcheson and Taylor maintained, that men still have this inherent virtuous inclination. Edwards asserted that Adam's nature shifted from virtuous to corrupt as a consequence of his sin and that all mankind became from that moment equally corrupt. Taylor contended, in opposition, that Adam's inherent disposition never at any time differed from that of the rest of mankind, and that most people have more good in them than bad. To Edwards, the doctrine of original sin, implying a fixed inclination to evil, goes hand in hand with the doctrine of necessity. Paradoxically, to prove that everyone else is determined, Edwards maintained that Adam was free. Taylor, on the other hand, denied original sin and attributed free will to absolutely everyone.

Edwards' main contention was that every human heart has a corrupt disposition. Whatever good exists, he attributed to the special working of grace. According to his argument, "he who commits any one sin, has guilt and ill desert so great, that the value and merit of all the good which it is possible he should do in his whole life, is as nothing to it." In a witty, although not very precise analogy, he observed that one should not argue that a wife is good because she performs the duties of a wife more frequently than she commits adultery.

As we have already pointed out, Edwards made no effort to prove his contention of man's depraved nature beyond his twofold method of appealing to Scripture and refuting Taylor's reasoning. More than half of his treatise is epitomized by such comments as: "The Scriptures are so very express upon it." Edwards assumed that if he could show that the doctrine is actually in the Bible and that Taylor's reasoning is frequently faulty, he would be proving that the doctrine presents the truth about human nature. Such an assumption makes the victory too easy for Edwards. Taylor in his way was as naïve as Edwards. As an exponent of the school of benevolence, he had seriously urged his variant of the notion of "the fortunate fall," that death and all the other consequences of Adam's sin came as benefits to mankind to enable its members to lead better lives in the future.

Edwards, also, was pushed by his main contention into

[122]

some rather preposterous corollaries and inconsistencies. After denouncing all mankind as deficient in love and gratitude toward God, he affirmed that truly holy men—particularly the Old Testament saints—love God more than sin. Literal interpretation of the Scriptures, of course, forced him into both conclusions. He was also drawn into some paradoxical statements about pagan religion, which, he maintained, had not declined until after Old Testament times, not immediately after Noah. Since his main theme required that he denigrate mankind universally, he was somewhat at a loss to account for the high morality of the ancient Greeks, to which most learned men had given glowing praise. He grudgingly admitted that "the pagan philosophers, and inquisitive men, made great improvements in many sciences, and even in morality itself," but insisted that they were nevertheless deficient in religion. Even more strangely, Edwards repeated the arguments of the deists that knowledge of God was available to all men at all periods of time; but, unlike the deists, Edwards added that few men heeded this knowledge —a circumstance that to him was proof of the universal stupidity of man's nature. One may ask then how Edwards could be a rationalist and logician if he believed in universal human stupidity. In a subsequent chapter we shall take up the question of Edwards' relationship to the general eighteenth-century concepts of rationalism and enlightenment.

After devoting more than two-thirds of his treatise to insignificant tilting with Taylor, Edwards finally concentrated on the underlying problem, citing "the more thinking part of mankind every where, who often asked this question, *Whence comes evil,* moral and natural evil." Edwards attempted an answer as he met Taylor's main objection to the doctrine of original sin, that it is injurious to God in supposing him to be "the author of a sinful corruption of nature."

Taylor had alleged that the doctrine implies that corruption resulted from a positive influence, some quality infused to alter "the natural constitution, faculties, and dispositions of our souls." Edwards replied that there was no need to suppose any evil quality infused into human nature by any positive cause or to suppose that man is born with "a *fountain of evil* in his heart, such as is any thing properly *positive.*" Expanding an argument suggested in the treatise on will, he

[123]

affirmed that the mere absence of positive good principles or the withholding of a divine influence to impart and maintain good principles, "leaving the common natural principles of self-love, natural appetite, &c. to themselves, without the government of superior divine principles—will certainly be followed with . . . the total corruption of the heart."

Edwards' theory was that Adam was at first endowed with two sets of principles—one of an inferior kind which Edwards called natural and the other of a superior order which he called supernatural. The natural principles consisted of self-love, or those natural appetites and passions in which man exercised love of his own liberty, honor and pleasure. The superior comprised the "spiritual, holy, and divine, summarily comprehended in divine love; wherein consisted the spiritual image of God, and man's righteousness and true holiness." The latter were designed to dominate the natural principles, and while they reigned, they were the glory of man's nature. But when Adam sinned, they were withdrawn —and man lost this supernatural communion with God. The inferior principle of self-love and natural appetites now became dominant. The superior principle ceased just as wholly as light ceases in a room where a candle is withdrawn. "And as *Adam's* nature became corrupt, without God's implanting or infusing of any evil thing into it; so does the nature of his posterity."

In his miscellanies, Edwards presented this system in more philosophical terms, conforming to the generally-held moral theories of the time. He divided the will of man into two categories, the first a rational will "arising merely from a rational judgment of what is best for him," the second an appetite or inclination "arising from the liveliness and intenseness of the idea of, or sensibleness of the good of, the object presented to the mind." The appetite struggles against the rational will and, in fallen man, overcomes it and keeps it in subjection. This division closely resembles the dichotomy of reason and passion assumed by Shaftesbury, Pope, Swift and other moralists. According to Edwards, man's whole will—comprising the dictates of both reason and appetite when they concur, or the dominance of one over the other when they disagree—is always free; but the rational will is not free, but subservient to the will of appetite. This is the difference between Adam and his posterity. Adam's rational will was free, as well as his inclinations. Adam's posterity, however, due to his fall, are dominated by the appetites or are servants of sin, in a theological sense, or under necessity in a philosophical sense.

In further theological terms, Adam had "sufficient grace" or an adequate freedom to act according to "the will that arose from a rational judgment of what was indeed best for himself." But God withheld "efficacious grace" or an irresistible power to resist all temptation he should meet with.

When Adam and Eve fell, their rational will was perverted and overcome by a deceived judgment, which, fitting in with an inferior appetite, overthrew the holy inclination to obedience. This holy inclination was at the same time diminished by their error of judgment in doubting that God would carry out what he threatened and in accepting Satan's suggestion that God had forbidden them the fruit out of unwillingness that they should equal him in honor and happiness.

Does this scheme imply in any way that God is the author of sin? In his treatise Edwards naturally tried to deny the general principle that God is responsible for evil, but admitted in practically the same terms he had used in the *Will* that "if for God so far to order and dispose the being of sin, as to *permit* it, by withholding the gracious influences necessary to prevent it, is for him to be the author of sin," then he would accept this consequence. His only explanation was that Taylor's system implied the same thing.

This is another place in Edwards' works where we have a right to be disappointed. Facing one of the most important theological questions he had ever raised—the problem of evil —Edwards resorted to evasion. Instead of bracing his philosophical muscles, he merely carped at his antagonist. The only fresh argument that Edwards advanced was to justify the continuation to Adam's posterity of his condition after the fall, that is, the rational will being dominated by the appetites. Edwards insisted that Adam's posterity's being born without holiness and so with a depraved nature comes to pass by "the established course of nature." The rest of his treatment is a repetition of the traditional Calvinistic position. Just as it is "agreeable to the established order of nature, that the good qualities wanting in the *tree*, should also be wanting in the *branches* and *fruit*," it is according to the order of nature "that since Adam, the head of mankind, the root of that great tree with many branches springing from it, was deprived of original righteousness, the branches should come forth without it." Edwards realized that the objection might be made that if flaws are imparted to the seed by the established order of nature, "why are not principles of holiness, when restored by divine *grace*, also communicated to *posterity?*" He answered by somewhat arbitrarily declaring that the work of Christ belongs to a different dispensation. "*Grace* is introduced among the race of man by a *new establishment;* not on the ground of God's original establishment, as the *head* of the natural world, and author of the first creation; but by a constitution of a vastly higher kind; wherein *Christ* is made the *root* of the tree, whose branches are his spiritual *seed*."

In his miscellanies, as part of a series of propositions and phenomena which he declared the reason of man is incapable of fathoming, Edwards took note that "both moral and natural evil abounds in the world." Experience had manifested "that great injustice, violence, treachery, perfidiousness, and extreme cruelty to the innocent abound in the world; as well as innumerable extreme sufferings, issuing finally in destruction and death." Like hundreds of philosophers before him, Edwards recognized that the ordering or permitting of this evil "in a world absolutely and perfectly under the care and government of an infinitely holy and good God, has a seeming repugnancy to reason that few, if any, have been able fully to remove." Edwards made no attempt at removing it himself, but in another part of his miscellanies he used reasoning that leads to the admission that God is directly responsible for moral evil. In a discussion of free will and man's power of attaining salvation, Edwards asserted the paradox that it is entirely in any man's power to submit to Christ as a savior, but that no man will ever do it unless he is impelled by God. In this sense, he affirmed, "all that men do in real religion is entirely their own act and yet every tittle is wrought by the Spirit of God." Presumably, in a discussion of evil, one must also admit the contrary: that all that men do of real evil is entirely their own act and yet every tittle is wrought by the Spirit of God. If confronted with this problem, Edwards would undoubtedly have raised his distinction between God allowing nature to take its course (producing evil) and his intervening in behalf of his chosen (producing salvation). Even with this distinction and the further granting that the evil nature in mankind came as a result of Adam's fall, the perpetuation of this evil would seem to be a positive act of God. In his treatise, Edwards argued that such a line of reasoning is parallel to objecting that the one who is the cause of the continuance in being of a man who has contracted vicious habits is to be considered the cause of his continued wickedness, and asserts that he is merely the cause of the continuation of the course of nature.

Whether the two conditions are really parallel depends on whether there is a fundamental difference between one man's suffering throughout his life the consequences of his own sin in an antecedent period and the entire posterity of one man bearing the taint or odium of its progenitor's sin and suffering the consequences of it. The opinion that the two conditions are exactly alike is affirmed in the doctrine of imputation— the view that God has imputed the guilt of Adam's sin to his posterity and that God is just and righteous in so doing.

This doctrine, regarding Adam as the "federal head" of the entire human race, is based on an analogy of a head and its body or a tree and its roots. Adam and his posterity were created organically united, according to Edwards, and the connection between them is exactly the same as though they had coexisted instead of living in various periods of time. Since Adam and his posterity "constitute but *one moral person*," all things with relation to evil disposition, guilt, pollution, and depravity, would exist, in the same order and dependence, in each branch, as in the root.

This is the doctrine. The next consideration is whether it is just and reasonable. Edwards' first argument on the affirmative side is the somewhat blunt assertion that there is no use blinking at facts—mankind is corrupt by nature and God does deal with Adam and his posterity as one. In unusually testy language, Edwards affirmed that "however the matter be attended with difficulty, *fact* obliges us to *get over* it, either by finding out some solution, or by shutting our mouths, and acknowledging the weakness, and scantiness of our understandings." He made no attempt whatsoever to deal with the objection that God seemed to weigh the scales against

Adam by allowing Satan a free hand. As Edwards himself presented the case, Adam's rational will was overcome not only by his appetite or inclination, but by the wiles of Satan, a being of superior intelligence. Edwards also refused to recognize that there could be any other alternative to considering every man singly for salvation, for example, endowing all men with a uniform, virtuous disposition. Edwards could not reject such a solution on the grounds that it would exempt man from a test of his moral qualities, for he had already repudiated Taylor's contention that there can be no merit without combat. He fell back, therefore, on the weak argument that posterity had greater advantage in having the issue rest in every man's being singly put to the test—that Adam might have stood fast in his obedience, and had he done so all posterity would have benefited. Edwards even thought it a valid argument to observe that Adam had the great advantage of being in the state of manhood when put to the test, whereas his posterity would be on trial from the moment they first became moral agents in childhood.

The crucial question is whether Adam and his posterity are actually one organic whole, or, in theological terms, whether the doctrine of Adam as a federal head is a tenable one. In answering it, Edwards drew upon the ontological speculation of his notebooks, basing his justification on his earlier solution to the problem of personal identity. According to his principles, the identity of consciousness in a single human being depends upon the immediate agency of God. As we have seen, Edwards believed that just as God is the infinite force or power that is constantly exerted to keep atoms together in the material world, so he is the force that creates continuity in individual consciousness. In the treatise on original sin, he argues that every created substance in being is upheld (or kept in existence) by the power of the Creator —not the antecedent existence of the same substance. For example, the present existence of the moon cannot be the effect of its existence at the last foregoing moment. "In point of *time*, what is *past* entirely ceases, when *present* existence begins." Therefore present existence cannot be an effect of past existence. God must cause every existence in each successive moment, a process "altogether equivalent to an *immediate production out of nothing*, at each moment."

[128]

Anyone who accepts this hypothesis concerning the moon would have no difficulty in granting that all existence, including that of every human being, depends upon the arbitrary constitution of the Creator, and that there is no identity or oneness in any creature except through God's decision to treat it as one. Obviously then, if God chooses to treat Adam's posterity as identical with Adam, this identity exists. "And all communications, derivations, or continuation of qualities, properties, or relations, natural or moral, from what is *past,* as if the subject were *one,*" Edwards claims, "depends on no other foundation." But even though we accept Edwards' premise that the nature of things amounts to an immediate production out of nothing at each moment, there is a serious flaw in applying it to the concept of identity. If identity depends on constant renewal or successive creation, what evidence have we of any principle of continuity whatsoever? In other words, why cannot the composition or identity of any parts of nature or even the whole be changed at whim at any moment? And if there is no certain continuation of identity in individual human beings, the entire federal concept of Adam and posterity falls apart. In a sense, Edwards answers this objection by affirming that "all oneness in created things, whence qualities and relations are derived, depends on a divine constitution that is arbitrary." But Edwards had set out to portray the federal concept as just and reasonable, not as completely arbitrary. Also, portraying the divine constitution as arbitrary amounts to the admission that God is the author of evil, a conclusion that Edwards had previously sought to refute.

Edwards' depiction of Adam's sin as the effect of an inherent disposition also indicts God as the exclusive fount of evil in the world—although Edwards was apparently unaware of the full consequence of his position. He actually affirmed that "the first evil disposition or inclination of Adam to sin, was not properly distinct from his first act of sin, but was included in it." Adam was, therefore, punished for the wickedness of his will, not the wickedness of the external act. This principle obviously defeats Edwards' contention that Adam's will was free. The logic of his treatise on the will would also serve to deny Adam's freedom. If every act of choice may be traced back through a chain of cause and effect to some cause outside the will, then Adam himself was also subject to this chain of cause and effect, and he was therefore so constituted that his sin was inevitable. In other words, his original sin was in the making before he committed it. And God rather than Adam was responsible.

Edwards admitted that God could have prevented Adam's evil disposition by the influence of his spirit, but this God withheld. And for this withholding, Edwards could offer absolutely no explanation or vindication. "Whatever mystery may be supposed in the affair," Edwards tamely insisted, "no Christian will presume to say, it was not in perfect consistence with God's *holiness and righteousness*." The critic will presume to say, however, that because Edwards failed to prove Adam's free agency and was unable to base the notion of Adam as a federal head on anything more reasonable than God's arbitrary will, he also failed to demonstrate that the doctrine of original sin is just, reasonable, or righteous.

Chapter 9

TRUE VIRTUE

Edwards fully realized that, in characterizing as evil practically all human motivation and behavior, he was writing against the prevailing temper of the times. He knew that deists such as Shaftesbury, latitudinarians such as Samuel Clarke, and moralists such as Hutcheson were affirming that if God be just, benevolent, and wise, he would endow his creatures with his own qualities of benevolence and virtue. Because of his intoxication with divine beauty and holiness, Edwards was attracted to the Shaftesburian thesis. At the same time, he also realized the incompatibility of the doctrine of original sin with "arguments, made use of by many later writers, from the universal *moral sense*, and the reasons they offer from experience, and observation of the *nature* of mankind, to show that we are *born* into the world with principles of *virtue;* with a natural prevailing relish, approbation, and love of righteousness, truth and goodness, and of whatever tends to the public welfare; with a prevailing natural disposition to dislike, to resent, and condemn what is selfish, unjust, and immoral; and a native bent in mankind to mutual benevolence, tender compassion &c." In an attempt to reconcile his own and the deists' notion of a benevolent God with the rigorous theology of Calvinism, Edwards planned twin treatises of cosmic morality: "The Nature of True Virtue," and "Concerning the End for which God Created the World." He wrote the first prior to his work on original sin and the second after it, but they were not published until after his death.

Unlike the treatises on the will and original sin, which Edwards conceived as polemics to bring others to his own way of thinking, and which were based on a ready-made system of doctrine, the treatises on virtue and creation were attempts to work out solutions to problems that Edwards himself had faced and on which his theology had imposed relatively few circumscribing dogmas. Although Edwards dutifully remarked that he had written both pieces to attack contemporary notions that tended "to corrupt Christianity," he did not single out any particular opponents for attack, and he treated opinions contrary to his own with great politeness—even those of the deists. He obviously did not consider these pieces as propaganda since, according to their first editor, they were intended for "learned and inquisitive" readers and their subjects were treated in a manner "something above the level of common readers."

The germ of Edwards' central ideas in both pieces may be found under the heading "Excellency" in his youthful notes on metaphysics that were compiled when he was first studying Locke. Here he enunciated the concept that all virtue is resolved into love of "being" in general. The spirit of his early conjectures is strongly Neoplatonic, conceived for example, in the bold declaration that we are emanations from God and that "in a being that is absolutely without any plurality, there cannot be Excellency, for there can be no such thing as consent or agreement." He also attempted a structural analysis of physical beauty, resolving it into equality, proportion and similarity of one being to another. In his later, printed treatises, he played down Platonism and substituted the esthetic theories of Hutcheson for his own analysis.

The second major source of the printed treatises is Edwards' manuscript collection of emblems, embodying the notion that the created world of nature reveals analogies with a spiritual world, and that fundamental truths concerning the attributes of God may be obtained through the rational perception of these analogies. Edwards earnestly held this concept as serious truth, not as poetic fancy. Variants of the title under which Edwards' emblems have been published, *Images or Shadows of Divine Things* (referring to the world about us), appear in both Edwards' youthful notes on metaphysics and in his mature treatises. Indeed we shall see that in the treatise on virtue, he paraphrases the one emblem that best summarizes the basic philosophical contention of the whole collection.

The third major source of the two treatises was the benevolent philosophy of Shaftesbury and Hutcheson. In the first section of his work on creation, Edwards noted that "Virtue, by such of the late philosophers as seem to be in chief repute, is placed in public affection, or general benevolence." He had long held a regard for affection (witness his treatise on *Religious Affections*); now, faced with the Shaftesburian dictum that virtue is affection, he was forced to decide whether such a notion is compatible with Calvinism. He concluded that the doctrine is erroneous only by being incomplete—that virtue has the nature of affection, but its object must be God rather than the public welfare. Essentially, both of Edwards' treatises represent an attempt to reconcile Calvinism with the fashionable theories of benevolent affections. In no sense was this a change in Edwards' basic thought, but merely a new emphasis of a particular aspect. He agreed with the concept of a benevolent universe but rejected the view of the deists that God's ultimate end was the happiness of his creatures. To Edwards, the ultimate end was God's own glory.

In writing on the will, Edwards had based his deterministic argument on psychological observation, and in treating original sin he had argued from Scriptural authority. But in discussing God's end in creation, he was in the realm of pure theory. To be sure, he had forerunners such as Samuel Clarke, who in his *Being and Attributes of God* had transcended the observable universe to read the divine mind. But in the main, Edwards had reason, logic, and imagination, as his only evidence or authority.

As an initial step, Edwards made a distinction between a supreme end, which is primary and unique, and an ultimate end, which may exist among several others and may be subordinate to another. This distinction enabled Edwards to ascribe different motives for God's creating and his governing of the world. His own glory was the motive of creation— the primary end—but after creation justice became the motive of governing—an ultimate end. Only after the creation did God bind himself to his creatures by his promises. Like all Puritans, Edwards was obsessed by covenants or contracts —and this distinction between primary and secondary ends

[133]

provided a justification for his notion of the covenants between God and man that filled his sermons.

Edwards next put forth the concepts that God referred to himself in his creation of the world, that God may value that which is good and valuable in itself (his own attributes), and that God could have no dependence on his created beings and could therefore not profit from them in any sense or receive anything from them. Then Edwards proceeded directly to a consideration of what are actually the effects of the creation that are in themselves valuable, without entering, as he expressed it, "on any tedious metaphysical inquiries, wherein fitness, or amicableness consists." These valuable effects consist in giving God occasion to exercise his power; allowing his attributes to be made known to other beings besides himself; enabling him to be loved and valued through the affection of other beings; and providing scope for his goodness to be expressed to the greatest degree. The latter is the concept of plenitude that A. O. Lovejoy has traced to ancient Greek sources in his masterly study of *The Great Chain of Being*. Edwards used the phrase "diffuse his own FULNESS," defined it as signifying "all the good which is in God natural and moral," and attributed it to the apostle Paul. In summary, "a disposition in God, as an original property of his nature, to an emanation of his own infinite fulness, was what excited him to create the world; and so, . . . the emanation itself was aimed at by him as a last end of the creation." Since Edwards' chief disagreement with Shaftesbury concerns the object of benevolence, denying Shaftesbury's contention that virtue consists in benevolence toward other beings, Edwards could not very well affirm that benevolence toward his creatures was God's object in creation. Edwards, therefore, compared God's disposition to a tree putting forth branches or the sun shining—the emanation of his own fullness. God's original object could not have been benevolence to the creature since the creature did not exist. But after creation, as a subordinate end, God was able to exercise his benevolence for the sake of the created beings themselves.

Edwards next took up the question of the manner in which God manifests a supreme and ultimate regard to himself in his works. For Edwards, this was another way of inquiring, how does God manifest himself to human beings and how should they respond to his revelation? Edwards concluded that God reveals knowledge of himself (reflected by men in conformity to God), God reveals his virtue and holiness (reflected in his creatures, as partaking of divine nature), and God reveals his happiness (reflected in his creatures, as enjoying and rejoicing in God).

Since the essence of Edwards' entire theological system is the concept of God's magnificence and glory, he was faced with the problem of attributing to God a pleasure in benevolence toward his creatures without suggesting that God has any need for subordinate beings or dependence on them. Edwards got around the difficulty by affirming that God may have pleasure in seeing the happy state of his creatures, even though his delight in himself is infinite. As God delights in his own beauty, he must at the same time delight at the reflection of it in his creatures' holiness. The latter is a participation of God's own beauty "as truly as a brightness of a jewel, held in the sun's beams, is a participation or derivation of the sun's brightness." This emphasis on God's independence and pleasure in manifesting a supreme and ultimate regard to himself in all his works raises another objection—that it dishonors God by portraying him as selfish. Edwards answered that God is actually generous and the opposite assumption indicates faulty reasoning. In the true sense of the word, selfishness is the pursuance of a small interest to the neglect of a great; generosity, the opposite spirit, is preference for the broad interest rather than the narrow. The latter is merely giving things their true value. Since God is the epitome of excellence, it is fitting that he should value himself more than his creatures. Although private interest may be contrary to public welfare in human relationships, it cannot be so with respect to the Supreme Being. "It is more absurd to suppose that his interest should be opposite to the interest of the universal system, than that the welfare of the head, heart, and vitals of the natural body, should be opposite to the welfare of the body."

Edwards' insistence on God's independence of his creatures threatened the Calvinistic view of the personal relationship between God and man—God's selecting certain individuals for preferred treatment and requiring prayer and praise from all his creatures. Lest his God seem too aloof, like that of the deists, Edwards was forced to make provision for reciprocal affection. To justify God's demand for man's worship, he applied the principle that all that is inherently excellent must be valued and delighted in. By analogy, if it becomes us to love our country and our friends and seek their being valued, it becomes God to seek that his own attributes should be valued and approved. And as for God's attitude toward his creatures, his love toward himself and his love toward others are not to be distinguished between as self-love and love toward others are in man—with God they are the same thing. God and his creatures, according to Edwards, are never to be viewed as opposite parts of a disjunction. "God's respect to the *creature*, in the whole, *unites* with his respect to *himself.*" Edwards was in the grip of a dilemma. He could not afford to make God appear too aloof on one side; nor could he, on the other, attribute to God too much concern for humanity, lest he be accused of adopting the Shaftesburian scheme of benevolence. The only possible solution was to declare that God's love for himself and that for humanity were the same—but God's supreme end was his own glory. On another level, Pope had said almost the same thing:

> Thus God and Nature link'd the gen'ral frame,
> And bade Self-love and Social be the same.

In resolving the apparent conflict between self-love and beneficence, Edwards affirmed that there are only two ways in which doing good to others from self-love may be inconsistent with the broader perspective of general benevolence. The first is acting from confined self-love or selfishness; the second, acting from dependence on others for the good we ourselves need or desire. "In some sense, the most benevolent, generous person in the world, seeks his *own happiness* in their good." But it is impossible for the Divine Being to partake of confined selfishness or feel a love contrary to general benevolence, for the simple reason that "he comprehends all entity, and all excellence, in his own essence."

In the dissertation on *The Nature of True Virtue*, Edwards combined moral with esthetic concepts in the vein of Shaftesbury and the seventeenth-century Platonists. At the outset, he defined virtue as the beauty of acts with a moral nature, something belonging to the disposition, will or heart as distinguished from the beauty of the understanding or the beauty of the countenance or body. True virtue, or the highest beauty, consists in benevolence to "being"—God, every person, and everything in general—and no love to anything less than all is true virtue. In other words, although love to any part of being—whether one person or all of humanity—may still be beauty, it is an inferior kind of beauty and is not true virtue. This concept Edwards had outlined, but not developed, in his youthful notes on Excellence. The extraordinary thing, which Edwards does not seem to have realized himself, is that his prescription for true virtue is exactly equivalent to the standard which he had ascribed to God—that God loves or values his own excellence and that his "respect to the *creature*, in the whole, *unites* with his respect to *himself*." In other words, the "true virtue" that Edwards was defining for his fellow human beings was the same attitude that he had attributed to God.

Reason tells us, Edwards argued, that the first object of a virtuous benevolence is being in general. This in itself will lead to the good of every individual, "unless it be conceived as not consistent with the highest good of being in general," in which case the inferior good will be given up for the higher. If being in general be the object of virtuous benevolence, then that that has the highest degree of existence will have the greatest share of this benevolent propensity. Edwards made absolutely no attempt to explain how Satan fits into this formula. The second object of virtuous benevolence is benevolent being in itself. "When any one under the influence of general benevolence, sees another being possessed of the like general benevolence, this attaches his heart to him, and draws forth greater love to him, than merely his having existence." Both objects, of course, represent God.

Edwards recognized that his theory of benevolence was compatible with prevailing opinion. "It is abundantly plain," he affirmed, "by the Holy Scriptures, and generally allowed, not only by christian divines, but by the more considerable Deists, that virtue most essentially consists in love. And I suppose, it is owned by the most considerable writers, to consist in general love of benevolence, or kind affection." The only basic difference between Edwards and the writers he had in mind consisted in his distinction, which other writers did not make, between true virtue and benevolence to a private system. According to this distinction, true virtue consists entirely in "cordial agreement" with being in general, and primarily and most essentially in supreme love to God. Any love more confining than being in general—including love of family or of country—is not true virtue. In Edwards' sense, the greatest love is that among the persons of the Trinity.

To allow for Scripture passages that indubitably exalt human love, Edwards granted that "it is sufficient to render love to any created being, virtuous, if it arise from the temper of mind wherein consists a *disposition* to love God supremely." But in the rest of his treatise, Edwards treated benevolence to mankind and other virtues depending on it as a kind of secondary and inferior beauty. In so doing, he reviewed his youthful esthetic theories in the light of the concepts of Hutcheson and other contemporaries.

Edwards defined secondary beauty, as "a mutual consent and agreement of different things, in form, manner, quantity, and visible end or design; called by the various names of regularity, order, uniformity, symmetry, proportion, harmony, &c." This beauty is an image of primary beauty, Edwards believed, but it could exist even in inanimate objects. In his use of the term beauty, Edwards assumed, without drawing attention to his assumption, that the good and the beautiful are the same. He took the concept for granted without even enunciating it as a principle.

Secondary beauty might consist in the agreement of the various sides of a geometrical figure as well as the parts of the human body. In his youthful notes on excellency, Edwards had attributed all physical beauty to equality and likeness of ratio, taking no notice of variety or irregularity. In his treatise, he cited Hutcheson's formula of "uniformity in the midst of variety" in an off-hand manner, without attempting to show how it could be reconciled with his notion of agreement. He also followed Bishop Berkeley in contending that the "beauty which consists in the visible fitness of a thing to its use, and unity of design, is not a distinct sort of beauty" from uniformity in the midst of variety. Here Edwards went contrary to Hutcheson, who had argued against Berkeley that we find beauty only in similitude of parts, even though unlike parts

would be equally useful. Edwards attempted to reconcile the
two views by declaring that a double beauty would exist in
an object with proportion in design that is at the same time
perfectly adapted to its use. The uniformity of two or more
pillars in different places, for example, would be less beautiful than the uniformity of pillars in the same building.

Edwards also pointed out that uniformity and proportion
affect the mind more in great objects than in small; for example, we are more greatly moved by the solar system than
by a tree or flower, by a cathedral than by a jewel box. Edwards' most fundamental departure from Hutcheson concerns
the connection between natural objects and a sentiment of
beauty. Hutcheson maintained that the connection was arbitrarily imposed by God, who could have formed us so as to receive no immediate pleasure from the regular forms, actions
and theorems that we now account beautiful, and could have
united pleasure to quite contrary objects. Edwards em-
phatically denied that the temper or disposition "whereby
the mind is disposed to delight in the idea of true virtue, is
given *arbitrarily,* so that if he had pleased he might have
given a contrary sense and determination of mind, which
would have agreed as well with the necessary nature of
things." Edwards, like Shaftesbury, regarded beauty as an
absolute quality, conforming to an invariable law in nature
in consequence of which all rational beings perceive beauty
in certain relationships and deformity in the contrary. The
theory of an arbitrary connection contradicts Edwards' principle that the essence of virtue consists in agreement or consent of being to being, for it implies that there is nothing in
the nature of things to hinder an exactly contrary temper of
mind agreeing as well with the nature of things. Edwards
held this supposition to be an absurdity and a contradiction,
for if virtue be an agreement of being to being, a temper of
mind agreeing to being in general must agree better with
general existence than a temper of opposition and contrariety
would agree with it.

When Edwards affirmed that secondary beauty is an image
of the true, spiritual, original beauty, one might think that
he was merely enunciating a final cause in the manner of
Addison. But when we are aware of his manuscript collection
of emblems, we realize that his system of esthetics is based

[139]

entirely on the notion of types and antitypes. "It pleases God to observe analogy in his works," asserted Edwards. We can now say with more assurance that it pleased Edwards to observe analogy in God's works. Edwards had discovered innumerable examples of God's establishing inferior things with analogy to superior. He observed in his treatise:

> In how many instances has he formed brutes in analogy to the nature of mankind! and plants, in analogy to animals, with respect to the manner of their generation, nutrition, &c. And so he has constituted the external world in analogy to the spiritual world, in numberless instances; as might be shown, if it were necessary, and here were a proper place for it.

In his emblem book, Edwards used almost the same words:

> If there be such an admirable analogy observed by the creator in His works through the whole system of the natural world, so that one thing seems to be made in imitation of the more perfect, so that the less perfect is as it were a figure or image of the more perfect, so beasts are made in imitation of men, plants are [a] kind of types of animals, minerals are in many things in imitation of plants. Why is it not rational to suppose that the corporeal and visible world should be designedly made and constituted in analogy to the more spiritual, noble, and real world? It is certainly agreeable to what is apparently the method of God's working. [No. 59]

For a complete understanding of the relationship that Edwards conceived between the secondary beauty of the material world and the primary beauty of the spiritual world, one would need to read his entire collection of emblems. But one or two give some idea:

> The silk-worm is a remarkable type of Christ, which when it dies yields us that of which we make such glorious clothing. Christ became a worm for our sakes, and by his death kindled that righteousness with which

believers are clothed, and thereby procured that we should be clothed with robes of glory. . . . [No. 35]

The revolutions of the spheres of the heavens are a great representation of the revolutions of the wheels of providence. And in the system of the world, there is a wheel in the midst of a wheel, the lesser spheres within the greater making several revolutions while the greater make one; and there are the revolutions also of the satellites, that are like a lesser wheel joined to a greater, making many lesser revolutions, while the greater makes one, very aptly representing the manner of things proceeding in divine providence. . . . The revolutions of the wheels of providence are aptly represented by the revolutions of the heavenly bodies, for they are those that rule the times and seasons, and are given for times and for seasons, and for days and for years, and hereby and by their secret influences on sublunary things, represent the angels, the ministers of God's providence. . . . [No. 154]

Edwards felt that perception of the analogies between one part of the universe and another produces a type of esthetic pleasure. Moreover, the kinds of secondary beauty that have the greatest resemblance to the primary, particularly the harmony of sounds and the beauties of nature, "have a tendency to assist those whose hearts are under the influence of a truly virtuous temper, to dispose them to the exercises of divine love, and enliven in them a sense of spiritual beauty." Yet Edwards also maintained that the pleasure that human beings derive from secondary beauty comes from an instinct or mechanical disposition, for, unlike God, they do not ordinarily perceive "that particular agreement and proportion, which . . . is the ground and rule of beauty in the case." A man who enjoys a pleasing tune, for example, may be completely ignorant of the theory of vibrations or scales. Also men do not reflect on the resemblance that secondary beauty has to primary.

In enunciating the principle that secondary beauty exists in immaterial things as well as in material, Edwards prepared the ground for his paradoxical rejection of human benevolence and ethics as below the standard of true virtue. Virtues such as order in society, wisdom, and justice, he maintained, are merely kinds of secondary beauty. "There is a beauty in the virtue called *justice*, which consists in the agreement of different things, that have relation to one another, in nature, manner, and measure; and therefore is the very same sort of beauty with that uniformity and proportion, which is observable in those external and material things that are esteemed beautiful. . . . Most of the duties incumbent on us, if well considered, will be found to partake of the nature of *justice*." Here in a nutshell is the ethical basis of Godwin's *Political Justice*. The secondary kind of beauty is also the foundation, according to Edwards, of William Wollaston's system that "resolved all virtue into an agreement of inclinations, volitions, and actions with truth."

The crucial question is, of course, the relationship in the individual between his true virtue and his secondary virtue. Although Edwards makes no clear commitment, he suggests that some human beings (those under grace)—as well as God—may exemplify true virtue. Presumably all normal human beings possess some degree of secondary virtue. Can this secondary virtue have any effect in producing true virtue? When trying to undermine secular notions of benevolent affections, Edwards insists that secondary beauty has nothing of the nature of true virtue. "A *taste* of this kind of beauty is entirely a different thing from a taste of true virtue." As other critics had done, Edwards pointed out the fallacy in the Shaftesburian equating of a moral sense with a sense of beauty: a disposition to approve the harmony of good music or the beauty of a geometric figure has nothing to do with rectitude or honesty in conduct. Otherwise a "delight in the beauty of squares, and cubes, and regular polygons . . . would increase in proportion to men's virtue . . . ; but would be almost wholly lost in some others that are very vicious and lewd." Yet if beauty and morality are not inherently connected, what becomes of Edwards' favorite doctrine of the analogy of material things to spiritual things? Indeed he almost rejects it by observing that material things "can have no more than a shadow" of such an analogy, and even though the analogy exists, he insists, man's appreciation of secondary beauty is not caused by knowledge of the analogy.

In the rest of his treatise, Edwards defines the moral value of all the dispositions in mankind that he categorizes as inferior to true virtue. This is the most valuable, if not the most influential, section of his work, particularly the extension of his remarks on self-love from his treatise on creation. According to Edwards, self-love may refer to two different things—to the normal expression of a natural capacity to experience pleasure (natural self-love), or to the preference of one's own pleasure over the welfare of anything else (narrow self-love). Loving what is pleasing means merely that a man has the capacity to love something, a capacity which distinguishes him from a stone. In this sense, self-love refers merely to the existence of inclinations and appetites prior to their being gratified. Among these are the benevolent affections, which have some virtue, although of the secondary kind, and these are the bases of natural self-love. Usually, however, self-love refers to the private, narrow interest that places individual welfare higher than that of any other person. Some liking for other people, friends, and family proceeds from this inclination, which has no virtue of any kind. By making this distinction between natural and narrow self-love, Edwards clearly rejected the selfish system of Hobbes, which placed all human motivation on the same level, and in this sense, as Shaftesbury had pointed out, supported the Calvinistic doctrine of natural depravity. Edwards also parted company, however, from Shaftesbury's opinion that the passions of gratitude and anger are based on moral sense and are therefore virtuous. All that is involved in these passions, Edwards affirmed, is a sense of desert, which is part of the secondary beauty of justice. Gratitude may be a noble principle in itself, but some gratitude may stem from narrow self-love just as it is possible for men to hate evil people and love good ones entirely out of self-love.

Having in some measure rescued self-love from the disesteem in which it was generally held, Edwards proceeded to do the opposite for natural conscience and moral sense— to label them as inferior principles. According to his opinion, a realization that one's conduct is contrary to nature has nothing of the primary beauty of true virtue, but represents merely a recognition of agreeing or disagreeing because of a natural principle. We always put ourselves in the other's place in order to judge our own conduct, a process so habitual that we hardly realize that it is taking place. Conscience, Edwards argued, consists of two parallel processes: (1) approving or disapproving conduct by the standard of what we would expect if we were in the other person's place; (2) approving or disapproving by a sense of desert. These two kinds of judgment give mutual support, one being founded on the other. Edwards' natural conscience extends to all virtue and vice; it may even approve true virtue by discerning the uniformity, equality and justice that it contains, but it does not see or taste the essence of true virtue, consisting in the union of heart to being in general.

Edwards attempted to prove his theory that natural conscience and virtuous disposition are not the same by citing the prevalence of sin. If the two were the same, a man's conscience would keep him from sin, but in reality many men whose consciences rebuke them strongly for their wickedness nevertheless persist in it. Edwards carried this argument to a truly ridiculous extremity by citing the day of judgment: if natural conscience and virtuous disposition were the same thing, sinners at the last day would acquiesce in God's punishment and their hearts would be changed to hate sin and love holiness; but Scripture teaches that, on the contrary, sinners shall rage in their hearts and their wickedness shall turn them into real devils.

The affectionate instincts are similarly void of true virtue. According to Edwards' view, an instinct is a natural disposition toward certain objects or actions: for example, hunger, thirst, sex, benevolence and jealousy. Among the affectionate kind, paternal love and patriotism have been mistaken for true virtue. Edwards insisted that these instincts do not arise from general benevolence or public affection, nor do they promote the public weal in the broadest sense. He agreed with Hume and Hutcheson, however, that sex is more than sensual gratification. Because it played such a rich and pleasant role in Edwards' own life, he would be ungrateful to disparage it philosophically. He insisted, nevertheless, that there is nothing in it of general benevolence, but that it is implanted by God for the continuation of the race. Similarly, pity is an instinct that God has provided for the preservation of the race. Not only does it not, in itself, promote general benevolence, Edwards affirmed, but it may even consist with malevolence. Typically Edwards added a prediction that "in the world of punishment" there will be neither pity nor affection between the sexes or among parents and children.

In conclusion, Edwards explained why moral sense, natural conscience, and affectionate instincts have been erroneously taken for virtue. Although their nature is different, they ordinarily have the same effects—such as promoting the general good and restraining vice. But, Edwards warned, we should never be deceived by this resemblance since even self-love sometimes restrains men from wickedness and inclines them toward the seeking of virtue, "yet it is not itself true virtue, but is the source of all the wickedness that is in the world."

Oddly enough, Edwards ended his treatise on this rather bitter note, apparently out of keeping with the rest of the work, which is devoted to the essence of virtue rather than vice. A partial explanation exists in his manuscript notes, where he attributes to his grandfather, Solomon Stoddard, the best philosophy he had ever encountered concerning original sin: "that it is self-love, in conjunction with the absence of the image and love of God. . . . There is nothing in the actions we call sin, but only the same self-love that necessarily belongs to that nature, working and influencing from that superior principle [the spirit of God] that particularly belongs to our nature and that is necessary in order to the harmonious exercise of it." It would seem that the keystone of Edwards' treatise on beauty and virtue was actually the doctrine of original sin.

Like the deists, Edwards seems to have made a distinction between public and private religion. The deists believed that enlightened minds like theirs could dispense with a belief in immortality and scorn Christianity as a tissue of superstition, but that the masses of people would not adhere to any moral standard unless they were held in line by the Christian doctrine of future rewards and punishments. Similarly, Edwards as a philosopher taught determinism, but as an evangelist assumed free choice. As a philosopher, he limited virtue to love toward being in general, but in a series of sermons published posthumously as *Christian Love, as Manifested in the Heart and Life,* he preached "Charity, or Love the Sum of All Virtue," describing charity in its practical manifestations as love of God and of our fellow creatures. In the same work he preached "Charity, or Love, More Excellent than the extraordinary Gifts of the Spirit," and specifically described doing good to others as the major part of charity. In real life, the deists found men to be worse than they had portrayed them philosophically and assumed that the social order could be upheld only by appealing to their baser motives. Edwards found men to be better than he portrayed them philosophically and appealed to their higher motives when he stood before them in the pulpit.

Although Edwards' exalting of general benevolence over more narrowly confined affections had a clearly traceable and important influence upon later thinkers, it was in turn a reflection of a pattern of thought quite general in the eighteenth century. Edwards may not have known about the writers who anticipated his notions, but his basic principle had been widely debated long before he wrote his treatise. It all began with an innocent remark by Jeremy Taylor to the effect that the word *friendship* is not so much as named in the New Testament. The deist Shaftesbury then took up the theme and exploited the lack of attention to friendship as one of the deficiencies of Christianity, adding patriotism as a parallel virtue ignored by the Scriptures. These omissions, Shaftesbury suggested, weaken the case for divine inspiration of the New Testament. Surprisingly, the allegations about friendship and patriotism became one of the focal attacks of the outraged divines upon Shaftesbury's *Characteristics*, "the deists' Bible."

The defenders of Christianity took two completely opposite positions: first, that friendship and patriotism are indeed specifically enjoined in the New Testament; second, that friendship and patriotism were deliberately passed over by Christ in favor of universal love, benevolence, or Christian charity, which encompassed and surpassed the two minor virtues. A typical example of the first defense is a sermon by Edwards' friend and fellow evangelist, George Whitefield, who exposed Shaftesbury's "horrid blunder" by pointing out that the epistles of John "show how christian friendship is to be cultivated" and that John, "the disciple whom Jesus loved," wrote private letters to his close friends. Surely if Shaftesbury ever read the Gospel, thundered White-field, "*having eyes he saw not, having ears he heard not:* but I believe the chief reason is, his heart being waxen gross, he could not understand; for . . . the world never yet saw such a specimen of steady disinterested friendship, as was displayed in the life, example, and conduct of Jesus Christ of Nazareth."

One of the most widely circulated defenses of the second type was James Foster's sermon, "The Christian Benevolence vindicated against the Objections of the Earl of *Shaftesbury.*" Foster argued that universal benevolence is enjoined by Christianity as the supreme law to all rational beings, and that it must not be superseded or weakened by any narrow or partial affections such as friendship or patriotism. This is the essence of Edwards' scheme.

The controversy even stimulated popular satirical poetry. Charles Churchill, in "The Farewell," 1764, presented a philosophical debate in which he defended patriotism and a poetic friend attempted in vain to exalt universal benevolence over it. The friend, following the familiar argument of universal philanthropy, asks whether patriotism is not really a vice which,

> . . . stops us in our course
> To that grand object of the human soul,
> That nobler love which comprehends the whole. . . .
> The gen'rous soul, by Nature taught to soar,
> Her strength confirm'd in philosophic love,
> At one grand view takes in a world with ease,
> And, seeing all mankind, loves all she sees.

Churchill, in his reply, was unique at this time in rejecting the concept of universal benevolence. In so doing, he anticipated the clamors against Godwin and the French perfectibilians, which came in reaction to the reforms of the French Revolution.

> Invented oft for purposes of art,
> Born of the head, though father'd on the heart,
> This grand love of the world must be confest

[147]

A barren speculation at the best.
Not one man in a thousand, should he live
Beyond the usual term of life, could give,
So rare occasion comes, and to so few,
Proof whether his regards are feign'd, or true.
The love we bear our country is a root
Which never fails to bring forth golden fruit.

Even though Churchill's "grand love of the world" and Edwards' "true virtue" are not exactly equivalent, the issues of the debates are identical.

The most bitter stage of the argument over narrow versus universal affections came in the wake of the subsequent publication of William Godwin's *Political Justice,* a work which pious souls in its day considered as immoral and pernicious. Like Edwards, Godwin established his system on a single principle, but instead of finding virtue in the love of being in general, Godwin held that nothing but love of the happiness of the greatest number of intelligent beings is virtue. What draws Godwin and Edwards even closer is their method of discrediting all other systems by their single principle. As Robert Hall, the most industrious nineteenth-century preacher against English infidelity, expressed it, "There is little doubt, from some parts of Mr. Godwin's work entitled *Political Justice* as well as from his early habits of reading, that he was indebted to Mr. Edwards for his principal arguments against the private affections: though, with a daring consistence, he has pursued his principles to an extreme from which that most excellent man would have revolted with horror."

Godwin himself acknowledged his debt to Edwards for the argument that gratitude, "if by gratitude we understand a sentiment of preference which I entertain towards another, upon the ground of my having been the subject of his benefits, is no part either of justice or virtue." The reason this acknowledgment particularly scandalized many pious readers of Edwards is that it appeared on the heels of one of the most notorious passages in *Political Justice,* the parable of Fénelon and his chambermaid. Designed to illustrate the principle that one man may be "a being of more worth and importance" than another, the parable presents Fénelon and his chambermaid in a blazing room and confronts the reader with the choice of which is to be saved. In keeping with the principle of both Edwards and Godwin, "that our love is always to be proportioned to the magnitude of its object in the scale of being," Godwin tells us that since Fénelon is of more worth than his chambermaid, his life is to be preferred. Even though we suppose the chambermaid to be our wife, our mother, or our benefactor, justice should teach us to prefer that which is more valuable—the life of Fénelon— at the expense of the other. We should never prefer our own parent or benefactor merely because of his kinship or benevolence to us. Gratitude is foreign to virtue and justice because it would lead to preferring one man to another from considerations other than that of his superior usefulness or worth.

Certainly Edwards' argument has nihilistic tendencies, and it is not strange that Godwin should have taken advantage of them—just as in defending necessitarianism he warmly endorsed Edwards' arguments against self-determinism and indifference. It is perhaps significant that Edwards' two most influential works, those on virtue and on the will, should have been attacked for sapping the foundations of Christianity. Robert Hall proclaimed that "many of the fashionable infidels" had hit upon a definition of virtue that perfectly coincided with that of Edwards, and an American minister, James Dana, who felt that the treatise on the will paralleled the views of celebrated ancient and modern infidels, circulated a report "that the english impression of Mr. Edwards on the will was promoted by the *deists* in London; and that the *rakes* in Holland had procured a dutch translation of it."

Chapter 10

REASON OR REVELATION

Certain thinkers, such as Godwin, who belong to the rationalist tradition of the eighteenth-century, have extracted single doctrines from Edwards' works and used them to erect systems completely alien to his supernaturalism. This rational-supernatural dichotomy persists among Edwards' followers. Joseph Haroutunian has acutely remarked that those critics impressed by Edwards' spirituality "have done no justice to his intelligence, and those impressed by his intelligence have been impervious to his 'sense of divine things.'" Edwards is most famous as a logician, but philosophers seem to concentrate on his idealism. Since he was the most eminent philosopher of the American enlightenment, one naturally wonders about his relationship to the broad ideals of the enlightenment concept. To what degree was he a rationalist? and to what extent did he accept the doctrine of progress?

According to a commentator of the nineteenth century, Edwards was the epitome of a rationalist. "So enormous is the development, so prodigious the superiority, of one particular faculty, that he might be almost said to possess *but* one. . . . It is, indeed, so obvious as to make it almost absurd formally to mention it. The character of his mind was essentially logical; the dominant attribute was REASON. He possessed probably in a greater degree than was ever before vouchsafed to man, the ratiocinative faculty." In analyzing Edwards' forensic method, the same critic observed that "he argues like a being without affections, a pure intelligence."

Edwards' notion of the manner by which knowledge is acquired certainly conformed with that of the scientific rationalism of the age. He wrote: "A common and steady effect shows, that there is somewhere a preponderation, a prevailing exposedness or liableness in the state of things, to what comes so steadily to pass. The natural dictate of reason shows, that where there is an effect, there is a cause, and a cause sufficient for the effect; because, if it were not sufficient, it would not be effectual; and that therefore, where there is a stated prevalence of the effect, there is a stated prevalence in the cause. A steady effect argues a steady cause. We obtain a notion of tendency, no other way than by observation: and we can observe nothing but events: and it is the commonness or constancy of events, that gives us a notion of tendency in all cases. Thus we judge of tendencies in the natural world." This is a statement that would have been endorsed by Benjamin Franklin and most other scientists and rationalists of the century.

But in addition to the processes of perception, observation, reflection and judgment implied in this description of reasoning, Edwards believed that knowledge may be acquired through intuition. We have already noticed the theory in his treatise on *Religious Affections*, and it is more explicitly stated in his earlier sermon on "The Reality of Spiritual Light." This is the theory that a supernatural light or increased awareness of the excellency in divine things is immediately imparted by God to the soul. "It not only removes the hinderances of reason, but positively helps reason. It makes even the speculative notions more lively. It engages the attention of the mind, with more fixedness and intenseness to that kind of object; which causes it to have a clearer view of them, and enables it more clearly to see their mutual relations, and occasions it to take more notice of them. The ideas themselves that otherwise are dim and obscure, are by this means impressed with the greater strength, and have a light cast upon them; so that the mind can better judge of them. . . . A true sense of the divine excellency of the things of God's word doth more directly and immediately convince us of their truth. . . . This is a kind of intuitive and immediate evidence." It is obvious that the comprehension Edwards is here discussing is religious comprehension and religious comprehension alone. Edwards consciously made a separation between secular and religious knowledge, arguing that the world has made great progress in the former—almost none in the latter. Reason by itself provides some knowledge of

[151]

religious truth, he taught, but this knowledge is entirely inadequate and must be supplemented by the more important instrument—intuition. Edwards never made the same application of a dichotomy of reason and intuition to secular knowledge and never gave a single illustration of the manner in which intuition may reveal knowledge of anything connected with the material universe. He did believe, however, that some ideas are innate: for example, the idea that every change in circumstances must have a cause.

In his *History of Redemption* Edwards rejoiced in the great increase in learning, "which began to revive with the Reformation, owing very much to the art of printing. . . . Since then, learning has increased more and more, and at this day is undoubtedly raised to a vastly greater height than ever it was before: and though no good use is made of it by the greater part of learned men, yet the increase of learning in itself is a thing to be rejoiced in, because it is a good, and, if duly applied, an excellent handmaid to divinity." Yet in his work on *Original Sin*—a more pejorative view of mankind —Edwards included a chapter on man's "proneness to an exceeding *stupidity* and sottishness in those things wherein his duty and main interest are chiefly concerned." His two examples were idolatry and "a general, great *disregard of eternal things*." It is not, he affirmed, "because the faculty of reason, which God has given to mankind, is not sufficient fully to discover them," that men do not observe the principles of religion and morality, but because of a wretched depravity of nature. Edwards was not alone in recognizing the disparity between man's attainments in secular learning and his deficiencies in morality or spirituality. Benjamin Franklin, in a famous letter to Joseph Priestley, regretted being born so soon because of "the rapid Progress true Science now makes," but ardently wished that "moral Science were in as fair a way of Improvement."

In posthumously published *Miscellaneous Observations on Important Theological Subjects*, Edwards raised the question "whether nature and reason alone can give us a right idea of God, and are sufficient to establish among mankind a clear and sure knowledge of his nature." His answer, as might be expected, was negative—that reason or the light of nature does not, as the deists maintained, furnish a knowledge of

God. Basing his exposition on Philip Skelton's *Deism Revealed*, Edwards affirmed, "There never was a man known or heard of, who had an idea of God, without being taught it." In other words, revelation is absolutely and vitally necessary for this knowledge. Edwards even quoted Skelton's astounding and significant admission that reason without the Bible would lead to materialism and Manicheanism: Granting that "every man is able to demonstrate to himself, that the world, and all things contained therein, are effects, and had a beginning"—and there is reason to doubt that unassisted reason would carry a man even this far—"yet if effects are to be ascribed to similar causes, and a good and wise effect must suppose a good and wise cause, by the same way of reasoning, all the evil and irregularity in the world must be attributed to an evil and unwise cause. So that either the first cause must be both good and evil, wise and foolish, or else there must be two first causes, an evil and irrational, as well as a good and wise principle. Thus, man left to himself, would be apt to reason, 'If the cause and the effects are similar and conformable, matter must have a material cause; there being nothing more impossible for us to conceive, than how matter should be produced by spirit, or anything else but matter.'"

Edwards continued to follow Skelton in declaring that, were it not for revelation, there is not a single doctrine of what the deists called natural religion that would not be forever involved in darkness and doubts. "It is one thing, to see that a truth is exceedingly agreeable to reason, after we have had it explained to us, and have been told the reasons of it; and another, to find it out, and clearly and certainly to explain it by mere reason."

Strangely enough, in all his insistence upon the necessity of something greater than reason for religious knowledge, Edwards never alluded to the other anti-intellectual supposition in some of his works that the fundamental doctrines of Christianity do not require a high degree of sophistication or even literacy, but are adapted to the simplest minds, such as, for example, that of the four-year-old Phebe Bartlet.

One cannot say that Edwards belongs to the tradition of skepticism. The classical Pyrrhonists had rejected all knowledge that comes from reason or the senses, and the seventeenth-century fideists had gone through the same process of elimination in order to fall back on the authority of the Roman Catholic Church. Edwards, however, put theological knowledge and all other "articles of knowledge" in separate categories, rejecting reason in favor of revelation for theology and accepting it for everything else.

There are obviously some subjects discussed in theology that are not treated in Christian Scripture, for example, God's motives in creating the world, the subject of Edwards' last treatise. Since the theme is not broached in the Bible, Edwards in handling it was forced to fall back on "Places of Scripture that lead us to suppose," texts that provided him the basis for argument, or verses that could lead to appropriate corollaries. He was also required to vindicate the use of reason as a source of knowledge on the subject, and in so doing he virtually overthrew his previous arguments against the validity of reason in divinity. Although repeating his theme that without revelation man would never have come to any determination of who the author of the world is, Edwards added that the long-continued assistance revelation has given man has enabled him to "come to great attainments in the habitual exercise of reason." He proceeded, therefore, to explore the dictates of reason on his subject, before attempting to extract the same doctrines from Scripture. Similarly, in his miscellanies he had declared that there are deductions of reason possible from what has been said in Scripture "of the most mysterious matters" and that these deductions may be as safe and certain as those about the most obvious and easy matters. On this assumption he grounded most of his philosophical theology concerning the Trinity.

In his formal attempt in *Miscellaneous Observations* to demonstrate that reason is inadequate to provide all men with an insight into the essential truth of religion, Edwards was faced with the problem of accounting for the sublime notions of God found in the classical philosophers, particularly in Plato and Cicero. If they did not come from reason, where did they come from since they had existed prior to the Christian tradition? Edwards in his youth had worked out an ingenious answer to this question, and he used it as the basis of most of the antideistic passages in his subsequent works. According to his solution, God had revealed the essential truths of religion to Noah, and whenever they flourished before the Christian era, they may be traced back to this source. This notion was by no means original with Edwards, for it may be found in such diverse predecessors as Sir Walter Raleigh's *History of the World* and Samuel Wesley's epic poem, *Life of our Blessed Lord and Saviour Jesus Christ*. But Edwards gave it an unique interpretation. In his *Notes on the Bible* he linked, for example, God's self-description to Moses, *I am that I am*, to the stream of Greek philosophy. "Some of the heathen philosophers," he declared, "seem to have derived notions that they had of the Deity from hence. Plato and Pythagoras make the great object of philosophy to be Tò Ǒν, *that which is;* Tò ὄντωs, *that which truly is;* and also Tò αὐτο Ǒν, *being itself*." We have already noticed that in his notes on mind, Edwards used as illustration of his view that God and real existence are the same, the "names of the deity, Jehovah, and I am that I am!"

In his *Miscellaneous Observations,* Edwards took up the same argument as he found it in Skelton: Socrates, Plato and Cicero were so little inclined to the belief in a future existence that they were afraid to found ethical systems on it. But Plato's notions were "infinitely more sublime and nearer the truth" than those of his master because he had traveled to Egypt.

That the ancient philosophers had as good a notion as they had of God, Edwards maintained, was due more to tradition that originated in divine revelation than to human invention—although reason served to keep the tradition alive. According to Edwards, experience had amply demonstrated that mankind—instead of depending on the light of nature to find out a right idea of God and his laws—had once been well acquainted with both and had gradually and at length almost universally lost sight of them, "insomuch that idolatry as bad as atheism, and wickedness worse than brutality, were established for religion and law in all countries." Edwards does not seem to have wondered why the same argument could not have been applied to his own notion of revelation—why one might not object that once revelation had been given to man it did not shed a uniform light. Why is it that certain points of history were dark—and others—such as the Reformation and the Great Awakening—glowed brightly? If Edwards were

[155]

to answer—as he did not, for he never faced the problem—that God's intervention explains these periods, then he would be attributing man's knowledge neither to reason nor to revelation in the sense of Scripture tradition.

Edwards did make an attempt to answer another objection that was frequently raised by the deists: if the Scriptures were intended to convey light to all mankind so that the truths of religion could be perceived by even the weakest minds, why is it that they are filled with mysteries and apocalyptic visions? Edwards explained that the mysteries were intended to give Christian people "exercise for their pious wisdom and study" and to enable them to make progress in understanding the Scriptures "as the philosophical world makes progress in the understanding of the book of nature, and in unfolding its mysteries."

Even though Edwards could convince his readers not to believe the deists' notion that natural reason would bring about the general recognition of a divine being, he still had to dispose of the claim that revelation itself, before it can be accepted, must be submitted to the scrutiny of reason for approval or validating. He chose to examine the argument as it had been presented by one of the most brilliant of the deists, Matthew Tindal, in his *Christianity as Old as the Creation*.

Edwards' first step was to define reason as "that power or faculty an intelligent being has to judge of the truth of propositions; either immediately, by only looking on the propositions, which is judging by intuition and self-evidence; or by putting together several propositions, which are already evident by intuition, or at least whose evidence is originally derived from intuition." If one accepts this definition as a satisfactory statement of the process by which one acquires all one's ideas, one would seem to be a rationalist. Edwards obviously accepted his own statement, but he held one minor reservation concerning the universality of its application. Tindal had argued, as had Toland before him, that if reason must decide whether any pretended revelation is genuine, it must therefore pass on every doctrine and proposition contained in the pretended revelation. Edwards maintained, by a method of argument drawn partly from Locke and partly from the body of Christian apologists, that reason must indeed pass on every pretended revelation as a system, but that once the

[156]

system has been accepted in general, the particular doctrines that comprised it must be exempted from scrutiny.

The essence of the deists' argument is most simply stated in a sentence in Toland's *Christianity Not Mysterious:* "There is no Mystery [or doctrine contrary to or "above" reason] in Christianity, or the most perfect Religion; and that by Consequence nothing contradictory or inconceivable, however made an article of Faith, can be contained in the Gospel, if it be really the Word of God."

Toland and Tindal relied entirely on internal evidence; they maintained that one cannot verify a system *in general* without examining and approving its particular doctrines first. Edwards relied instead on external evidence, arguing that if such supports as miracles, prophecy, and tradition furnish proof of the truth of a system, the unreasonableness of any part must be considered a sign of the weakness or limitation of human reason rather than of a fault in the general system. Despite his idealistic philosophy and his knowledge of Newtonian physics, he still fell back on traditional apologetics, prophecy and miracles, as his best proof of Christianity.

The remainder of his arguments were intended to demonstrate the deficiencies of reason. "A proposition may be evidently true," he argued, ". . . though the particular propositions that depend upon it, and follow from it, may be such, that our reason, independent of it, cannot see the truth, or can see it to be true by no other means, than by first establishing that other truth, on which it depends." As examples, Edwards argued that we accept the proposition that we may believe the testimony of history and tradition, the testimony of those we see and converse with, the testimony of our memories, and the testimony of our senses; yet many of the truths that we accept as consequences cannot be known directly by reason. Edwards was a master of arguing by analogy, although some of his parallels are not very close. One wonders whether he really overlooked the obvious fact that Toland, in objecting to the particular propositions consequent to Christianity that fail to conform to reason, would have objected equally to any proposition consequent to the testimony of those we see and converse with, or to the testimony of history, that failed to conform to reason.

Edwards similarly argued that we accept on faith a great

deal of knowledge about the universe that we have not experienced and that we do not understand, for example, the effects of electricity and magnetism. Nature is full of mysteries; the further it is traced and observed, the more mysteries appear. The same is true of divine revelation, he maintained, and difficulties should not be held as arguments against it, but rather as confirmations or arguments in its favor. Furthermore, the difficulties attendant upon a revelation of spiritual nature will be vastly multiplied: the things of this world will be of a different kind from "the objects and affairs which earthly language was made to express."

Having used the method of analogy to demonstrate to his own satisfaction that God's revelation through nature involves almost the same complexity as God's revelation in the Scriptures, Edwards based his final argument on the twofold requisites of a satisfactory religious system. It must provide: "*1st,* The religion of nature, or the religion proper and needful, considering the state and relations we stand in as creatures; *2d,* The religion of a sinner, or the religion and duties proper and necessary for us, considering our state as depraved and guilty creatures, having incurred the displeasure of our Creator." However sound the logic may be in Edwards' other works, the second requirement, predicated on the doctrine of depravity in Calvinistic Christianity, the very system presumably being proved or vindicated, actually says nothing more than that no system of religion can conform to Calvinism except Calvinism.

One wonders whether, in any other realm, Edwards would have accepted general propositions from external evidence alone, without insisting that they be based on rationally acceptable subordinate propositions.

In vindicating revelation, nearly all of Edwards' inferences tended to depreciate reason. In *Religious Affections* he even disparaged the "external" arguments based on miracles and prophecy that he himself used elsewhere to support revelation against Tindal. Only in recent years, he affirmed, have these arguments "been set in a clear and convincing light, even by learned men themselves: and since it has been done, there never were fewer thorough believers, among those who have been educated in the true religion; infidelity never prevailed so much, in any age, as in this, wherein these arguments are handled to the greatest advantage."

Even though Edwards believed that the gospel "does not go abroad abegging for its evidence . . . it has its highest and most proper evidence in itself," he felt that great use may be made of "external arguments" to awaken unbelievers and confirm the faith of true saints. He also held fast to his primary notion that "there is no spiritual conviction of the judgment, but what arises from an apprehension of the spiritual beauty and glory of divine things." True saints, he affirmed, "can not only say, that *they think* the gospel is divine, but that *it is divine.*"

The truth is that Edwards did not believe that the highest religious or moral knowledge comes through reason. Nor did he believe that the particular doctrines of Christianity should be expected to conform to reason. Yet, as all skeptics do, he used reason and logic to reveal the deficiencies of reason. He also used reason to demonstrate propositions that, according to his own theory, are beyond the reach of reason.

It must not be overlooked that Edwards' favorite method of deriving knowledge through analogies or types in nature and in the Scriptures is something other than a rational process. Certainly it does not conform to the definition of reason contained in his answer to Tindal. Yet his emblems were intended to be used, eventually, in a projected *"Rational* Account of the Main Doctrines of the Christian Religion"—even though in his treatise on *Original Sin*, he ridiculed his opponents for having "tropes and figures multiplied, one upon another."

Edwards is a rationalist in the sense that the best passages in his forensic works reveal extraordinary powers of logic and nearly all of his writing gives the appearance of appealing to reason; but these appearances hardly overweigh the nonrational elements.

In regard to the doctrine of progress, Edwards held an ambivalent attitude, which varied according to the theological doctrine uppermost in his mind. When writing on the doctrine of original sin, Edwards maintained, as might be expected, that man as an innately evil creature can never outgrow his corruption. But when speculating on eschatology,

[159]

he assumed that the millennium was not only on the way, but not very far away.

Edwards considered the Reformation as a period of great light but since that time, he lamented, even the Protestant nations had been deluged with "infidelity, profaneness, luxury, debauchery, and wickedness of every kind." Things were in such an evil state throughout most of the Christian world that Edwards considered the "poor savage *Americans*" as mere babes in comparison to most nominal Christians "as to proficiency in wickedness." Even the people of New England had "forsaken the pious examples" of their fathers. When the Arminians maintained that the world was then enjoying a great advancement of light and truth, Edwards snapped back that "on the contrary, vice, and every thing opposite to practical Christianity, has gone on to increase, with such a prodigious celerity, as to become like an overflowing deluge."

But in his private miscellanies Edwards sang another tune. Most amazing of all, he used the image of water emptying into the sea both to deny and affirm progress. In his printed work on original sin, he declared that the world "makes little or no progress, after all its revolutions and restless motions, labours, and pursuits; like the sea, that has all the rivers constantly emptying themselves into it, from age to age, and yet is never the fuller." But in discussing the end of the world in his miscellanies, Edwards asked the rhetorical question: "Does God make the world restless, to move and revolve in all its parts, to make no progress, to labour with motions so mighty and vast, only to come to the same place again, to be just where it was before?" He confidently affirmed: "Doubtless some end is nearer approached to by these revolutions. . . . The waters of the sea are not so restless, continually, to ascend into the heavens, and then descend on the earth, and then return to the sea again, only that things may be as they were before."

Among his emblems, Edwards used the identical image to express a cyclical theory of history [No. 22], but he also included two others to designate progress:

The late inventions of telescopes, whereby heavenly objects are brought so much nearer and made so much plainer to sight and such wonderfull discoveries have

been made in the heavens, is a type and forerunner of
the great increase in the knowledge of heavenly things
that shall be in the approaching glorious times of the
Christian church. [No. 146]

The changing of the course of trade and the supplying
of the world with its treasures from America is a type
and forerunner of what is approaching in spiritual things,
when the world shall be supplied with spiritual treasures
from America. [No. 147]

Edwards even believed that the progress of the church in
heaven goes parallel with the progress of the church on earth
—and that the heavenly church depends on the earthly one!
We find this remarkable opinion in his notes on the Bible,
probably written during the flush of revival enthusiasm: "the
church in heaven, as to the progress it makes in its state of
glory and blessedness, keeps pace with the church on earth;
. . . the glory of both is advanced together; . . . the affairs of
the church in heaven, have some way or other a dependence
on God's providence towards his church on earth, and . . .
their progress is dependent on the progress of things in God's
providence towards his church here." Lest this not be an-
thropocentric enough, Edwards added that all the happiness
of the saints and angels in heaven depends on the progress
of God's providence on earth. The discoveries in the realms
of physics do not seem to have made such an impression upon
Edwards as some of his uncritical admirers believe.

Edwards most fully developed his millennial thought in
A History of the Work of Redemption, the piece that one
critic regards as the crown of Edwards' career. Here Edwards
defined redemption as "a work that God carries on from the
fall of man to the end of the world." When looking back to
the fall, Edwards was a pessimist and scoffer at progress—
when looking in the opposite direction, he was almost an op-
timist. Considering redemption as the entire Christian dispensation, Edwards celebrated the great works of God, giving
particular attention to the restoring of the ruins of the fall
of man, which he felt would culminate in the end of the
world. Although Edwards intended to perfect his history as
one of his projects at Princeton, the published version is based
on a series of sermons that he delivered in 1739. Another of

his works composed for the unlearned, it amounts to an eighteenth-century evangelical equivalent of H. G. Wells' *Outline of History*. In a sense, it can be considered the first venture in "thesis history" in the New World, about the best that can be said for it.

Edwards believed, when he issued his proposal in 1747 for joining the Scottish divines in praying for the advancement of God's kingdom, that his generation might be the one to see the Lord appear in his glory and build up Zion. This millennial wishful thinking is beautifully adapted to Edwards' scheme of theological idealism. If, as he maintained, all creation is nothing but an idea of God, and all things—past, present and future—are equally in God's consciousness, then a rigorously observed timetable for the end of the world could very well be a part of God's mental process.

Chapter 11

CONCLUSION

There is no more use in trying to explain Edwards' genius than Franklin's. Nothing in the preceding generations of his family or in his milieu suggests why he should have emerged as the greatest, and virtually the only, philosopher of the American colonies.

Yet for all his metaphysical eminence and leadership in the Great Awakening, Edwards had practically no enduring influence on the culture of his own or later generations. In the realm of applied religion he was superseded by Whitefield, and in the realm of theology he was not a dynamic force. He led the resistance to change for a time, but established no major school and imposed no new direction. Except for his classic treatises on the will and the affections, his works most highly regarded now are mainly those that were not published during his lifetime.

One biographer has maintained that if Edwards had not been a Calvinist, he would have been a greater, more influential, intellectual and spiritual leader. The truth is that Edwards rose to his dominating position among the theologians of his time only because he was a Calvinist. Otherwise there would have been no drive or direction to his work. Whether or not he was more at home with theological dogma than with abstract speculation, he allowed his speculation to be dominated by Calvinistic doctrine, which he accepted bodily.

Edwards loved God so much that, in describing the divine power, he merged it into the whole universe, not leaving a single atom separate from God for an instant. As a result, the distinction between the world and the superior intelligence directing it became lost. For this reason his works could be charged with pantheistical or atheistical tendencies. In addition, Edwards' great talent was a destructive one; he demolished all of the conventional arguments for free will and exposed the fallacies in most of the current systems of ethics. But he contributed little on the positive side.

His idealistic speculation cannot be considered a fundamental contribution. It played no part in his major treatises; it was not published during his lifetime; and it contains little not expressed by Edwards' predecessors or contemporaries.

Moreover, it is not true, as sometimes has been claimed, that Edwards was a pioneer in applying metaphysics to theology; one need mention only Wollaston, Butler, and Clarke. Edwards was a tireless and valiant defender of the Calvinistic system of theology, but with one possible exception his name has never been associated with a single original doctrine of philosophy or theology. The possible exception is his theory of religious affections, but he can hardly be given credit for creative originality in propounding it. He merely treated systematically and with encyclopedic thoroughness a concept that was already on the way to acceptance.

In the history of philosophy, Edwards belongs entirely to the stream of English writers. Although he knew Plato and the ancients, he shows no influence of Pascal, Descartes, or the two continental thinkers whose thought in some respects oddly resembles his, Spinoza and Leibniz. He was certainly more God-intoxicated than the first, and as convinced as the second that this is the best of all possible worlds. In the commonly accepted dichotomy of eighteenth-century English philosophy, Edwards openly followed Locke but was subconsciously drawn to Shaftesbury. The English journalist William Hazlitt once told a group of friends that there were only six philosophers of any value in modern times: Hobbes, Berkeley, Butler, Hartley, Hume, Leibniz, and possibly Jonathan Edwards, "a Massachusetts man," as a seventh. This classification does Edwards no injustice.

Four main characteristics stand out in Edwards' total work:

1) It represents a revival of mystical thought in the sense of conceiving God as Being-in-general, whose immediate power is known through intuition. Edwards' original contribution in this domain should not be exaggerated, for Berkeley, Shaftesbury, and Hutcheson had already upheld this tradition with distinction.

2) It represents the culmination of the systematic presentation of Calvinism in Anglo-Saxon countries, and virtually its last stand.

3) It is the most literate contemporary commentary in America on the principal theological issues of the eighteenth century. Edwards' views are always stimulating, even though frequently reactionary.

4) It epitomizes a recurrent psychological manifestation toward life (the sinner-revival complex), which in various forms is still with us.

Edwards' various works, or the different parts of his theological system, fit together like the parts of a jig-saw puzzle. His student speculations foreshadowed his mature treatises, and each one of the latter reflects in some way the basic idea of every other. Practically any one of his works could serve as a commentary on any other. But all that Edwards' extraordinary logical consistency really means is that he adhered rigidly to Calvinistic theology on which every part of his own system is based. If the doctrines of Calvinism fit together as a system, Edwards' philosophy can do no less.

Even then, Edwards sometimes wanted to have his system go in opposite directions: he declaimed with equal vehemence on the law of cause and effect, and God's immediate influence; the benevolence of the universe, and man's absolute depravity; and the great advance of learning and knowledge, and man's universal stupidity. And the main trouble with Edwards' doctrines, unusually consistent though they may be, is that they did not always seem to fit the experience of life and human nature.

Edwards' contemporary, Ezra Stiles, wrote in his diary that Edwards' writings in another generation would "pass into as transient notice, perhaps as scarce above oblivion, as Willar, or Twiss, or Norton; and when posterity occasionally comes across them in the rubbish of libraries, the rare characters who may read and be pleased with them, will be looked upon as singular and whimsical, as in these days are admirers of Suarez, Aquinas, or Dion. Areopagita." If Stiles' unflattering prediction has not come to pass, it is probably because (1) Edwards was the only American clergyman of his century to attain any kind of international reputation; (2) his philosophy has wider appeal than would be expected, for it curiously resembles that of his opponents, the deists, on many points, and (3) he has become the symbol of the American puritan.

SELECTED BIBLIOGRAPHY

A complete bibliography of early editions appears in Thomas H. Johnson, *The Printed Writings of Jonathan Edwards, 1703–1758; a Bibliography* (Princeton, 1940).

Collected Works

Austin, Samuel (ed.). *The Works of President Edwards.* 8 vols. Worcester, Mass., 1808–09.

Carter, Robert, and Brothers (eds. and publishers). *The Works of President Edwards.* 4 vols. New York, 1881.

Dwight, Sereno E. (ed.). *The Works of President Edwards.* 10 vols. New York, 1829–30. [The standard edition until supplemented by the Yale edition begun in 1957.]

Hickman, Edward (ed.). *The Works of President Edwards.* 2 vols. London, 1834.

Ramsey, Paul (ed.). *Freedom of the Will (The Works of Jonathan Edwards;* Perry Miller, gen. ed., Vol. I.). New Haven: Yale University Press, 1957.

Smith, John E. (ed.). *Religious Affections (The Works of Jonathan Edwards;* Perry Miller, gen. ed., Vol. II.). New Haven: Yale University Press, 1959.

Texts Not in Collected Works

Clark, G. P. (ed.). "Unpublished Letter of Jonathan Edwards." *New England Quarterly,* XXIX (June, 1956), 228–33. [To Rev. Peter Clark on the Northampton controversy.]

EDWARDS, TRYON (ed.). *Charity and Its Fruits, or Christian Love as Manifested in the Heart and Life.* London, 1851. (Reprinted as *Christian Love in the Heart and Life.* Philadelphia, 1875.) (Evidence of Edwards' humanitarianism.)

FISHER, G. P. (ed.). *An Unpublished Essay of Edwards on the Trinity.* New York, 1903. [A long introduction, followed by a short essay, adhering to orthodox theories of "tri-personality with the avoidance of tri-theism."]

GROSART, ALEXANDER B. (ed.). *Selections from the Unpublished Writings of Jonathan Edwards, of America.* Edinburgh, 1865. [Contains a "Treatise on Grace" and "Annotations on Passages of Holy Scripture."]

MILLER, PERRY (ed.). *Images or Shadows of Divine Things.* New Haven, 1948. (A collection of emblems or analogies between natural phenomena and doctrines of Christianity.)

———. "Jonathan Edwards on the Sense of the Heart." *Harvard Theological Review,* XLI (April, 1948), 123–45. [Contains a fragment of Edwards' "Miscellanies" adumbrating the epistemology of *Religious Affections.*]

———. "Jonathan Edwards' Sociology of the Great Awakening." *New England Quarterly,* XXI (March, 1948), 50–78. [Contains extracts from three sermons, rare instances of Edwards' recognition of social problems.]

PARK, EDWARDS A. (ed.). "Original Letter of President Edwards." *Bibliotheca Sacra,* I (August, 1844), 579–91. [To Joseph Hawley, Nov. 18, 1757.]

SMYTH, E. C. (ed.). *Observations Concerning the Scripture Economy of the Trinity and Covenant of Redemption.* New York, 1880. [Evidence that Edwards did not neglect the themes of Christology or the Trinity.]

TOWNSEND, HARVEY G. (ed.). *The Philosophy of Jonathan Edwards from His Private Notebooks.* Eugene, Ore., 1955. [The largest selection from Edwards' "Miscellanies" so far published.]

WILLIAMS, S. T. (ed.). "Six Letters of Jonathan Edwards to
Joseph Bellamy." *New England Quarterly*, I (April,
1928), 226–42. (On personal concerns.)

Selected Works

FAUST, CLARENCE H., and JOHNSON, THOMAS H. (eds.). *Jonathan Edwards, Representative Selections*. New York,
1935. [Contains excellent introduction, bibliography,
and notes.]

FERM, VERGILIUS (ed.). *Puritan Sage: Collected Writings of
Jonathan Edwards*. New York, 1953. [More extensive
selections and less scholarly apparatus than in the
Faust and Johnson volume.]

Biography and Criticism

Except for the most pertinent early works, this list is
limited to the twentieth century.

ALDRIDGE, A. O. "Edwards and Hutcheson." *Harvard Theological Review*, XLIV (January, 1951), 35–53.

———. "Jonathan Edwards and William Godwin on Virtue."
American Literature, XVIII (January, 1947), 308–18.

CADY, E. H. "The Artistry of Jonathan Edwards." *New England Quarterly*, XXII (March, 1949), 61–72. [Analysis
of the Enfield sermon to demonstrate that it is "a
genuine work of literary art."]

CARPENTER, F. I. "The Radicalism of Jonathan Edwards."
New England Quarterly, IV (October, 1931), 629–44.
[Finds parallels between Edwards and Whitman,
Robinson Jeffers, Dreiser, and William James.]

CRABTREE, A. B. *Jonathan Edwards' View of Man*. Walling-
ton, England, 1948. [A Zurich dissertation, presenting
Edwards' system in outline.]

ELWOOD, DOUGLAS J. *The Philosophical Theology of Jonathan
Edwards*. New York, 1960. [Attempts to show that
Edwards has more in common with twentieth-century
theology than with that of the eighteenth century;
in philosophical terms, revives the old view of Edwards
as a mystic.]

FAUST, C. H. "Jonathan Edwards as a Scientist." *American Literature*, I (1929–1930), 393–404. [Argues that scholars have exaggerated his scientific interests.]

GARDINER, H. N. (ed.). *Jonathan Edwards: A Retrospect.* New York, 1901. [Addresses on the 150th anniversary of his dismissal from Northampton.]

GERSTNER, JOHN H. *Steps to Salvation.* Philadelphia, 1959. [Excellent analysis of the thought of Edwards' sermons.]

GOHDES, CLARENCE. "Aspects of Idealism in Early New England." *Philosophical Review*, XXXIX (November, 1930), 537–55. [Shows resemblances to the thought of the Cambridge Platonists.]

HAROUTUNIAN, JOSEPH. "Jonathan Edwards: Theologian of the Great Commandment." *Theology Today*, XIII (October, 1944), 361–77. ["A prolegomenon to the theology of Edwards."]

———. *Piety Versus Moralism.* New York, 1932. [Traces the decline of Calvinism in New England.]

HOPKINS, SAMUEL. *The Life and Character of the Late Reverend Mr. Jonathan Edwards.* Boston, 1765. [A panegyrical biography by Edwards' friend and disciple.]

HORNBERGER, THEODORE. "The Effect of the New Science upon the Thought of Jonathan Edwards." *American Literature*, IX (May, 1937), 196–207.

JOHNSON, T. H. "Jonathan Edwards' Background of Reading." *Publications of the Colonial Society of Massachusetts*, XXVIII (1935), 193–222. [Indispensable for a study of Edwards' sources.]

McGIFFERT, A. C., JR. *Jonathan Edwards.* New York, 1932. [Shows the significance of Edwards' religious psychology.]

MILLER, PERRY. *Jonathan Edwards.* New York, 1949. [Intellectual biography, attempting to interpret Edwards as a precursor of modern thought.]

MILLER, SAMUEL. "Life of Jonathan Edwards." In *Library of American Biography*, conducted by Jared Sparks, Vol. VIII, New York, 1839. [Percipient treatment of social and intellectual background.]

Morris, William Sparkes. "The Reappraisal of Edwards." *New England Quarterly*, XXX (December, 1957), 515–25. [Excellent review of the first volume of the Yale edition of Edwards' works; points out that Edwards has been treated successively by theologians, philosophers, and students of American literature.]

————. *The Young Jonathan Edwards: A Reconstruction.* University of Chicago dissertation, 1955. On microfilm. [Attempts to demonstrate that Franciscus Burgersdicius and Adrian Heerebord, Dutch Calvinists, "supplied the major part of the metaphysical ideas of Edwards' heritage."]

Murphy, Arthur E. "Jonathan Edwards on Free Will and Moral Agency." *Philosophical Review*, LXVIII (April, 1959), 181–202. [Shows that Edwards demolishes not only freedom of the will, but the will itself, as well as the moral agency of man.]

Parkes, H. B. *Jonathan Edwards: The Fiery Puritan.* New York, 1930. [A lively, debunking biography.]

Rice, Howard C. Jr. "Jonathan Edwards at Princeton: With a Survey of Edwards Material in the Princeton University Library." *Princeton University Library Chronicle*, XV (Winter, 1954), 69–89. [Prints some Edwards letters and describes some volumes that he formerly owned.]

Tomas, Vincent. "The Modernity of Jonathan Edwards." *New England Quarterly*, XXV (March, 1952), 60–84. [A satirical protest against Perry Miller's method of treating Edwards' ideas to make them appear modern, and a defense of the contrary doctrine that Edwards was essentially a medieval philosopher.]

Townsend, H. G. "The Will and the Understanding in the Philosophy of Jonathan Edwards." *Church History*, XVI (1947), 210–20. [Traces these "two principal faculties of the soul" in Edwards' thought.]

Turnbull, Ralph G. *Jonathan Edwards: The Preacher.* Grand Rapids, 1958. [Emphasizes style and technique of sermons.]

WINSLOW, OLA E. *Jonathan Edwards.* New York, 1941. [The best biography.]

WRIGHT, CONRAD. "Edwards and the Arminians on the Freedom of the Will." *Harvard Theological Review,* XXXV (October, 1942), 241–61. [Points out that Edwards' followers failed to understand him and that the Arminians failed to realize that he had interpreted them incorrectly: essentially the two groups were closer together than they seemed to be. Instead of attacking moral necessity, the Arminians would have been on sounder ground to attack moral necessity as it was combined with total depravity, as presented in *Original Sin.*]

INDEX

A

Absolute necessity, doctrine of, 85-86

Account of the Late Reverend Mr. David Brainerd (Edwards), 43

Adam, Edwards on, 124-30

Addison, Joseph, *Spectator* paper (No. 413), 4

Affectionate instincts, 144-45

Affections, religious, 74-79, 158

Anderson, James, 13

Arminianism, 22, 23, 24, 80, 86; contingence concept and, 89-90; Edwards' assault on, 87-100, 105, 106; indifference concept and, 89, 90, 105; liberty and, 87; necessity and, 114-15; sin and, 89; virtue and, 87, 89

B

Bartlet, Phebe, 26, 153

Bayle, Pierre, 112

Beauty, 140; primary, 140, 141; secondary, 138, 139, 141

Being and Attributes of God (Clarke), 133

Bellamy, Joseph, 59, 61

Benevolence, theory of, 137

Berkeley, George, 164

Book of Nature and Common Providence and The Language and Lessons of Nature (Edwards), 16

Brainerd, David, 43-44

Bunyan, John, 2

Burr, Aaron, 61

Burr, Esther, 63, 64

C

Calvinism, 12-13, 17, 56, 80, 125, 165

Causation, doctrine of, 84, 86

Chauncey, Charles, *Seasonable Thoughts on the State of Religion in New England*, 32

Christian Love, as Manifested in the Heart and Life (Edwards), 145-46

Christianity as Old as the Creation (Tindal), 156

Christianity Not Mysterious (Toland), 157

Churchill, Charles, "Farewell, The," 147-48

Cicero, 154, 155

Clap, Thomas, 34

Clarke, Samuel, 131; *Being and Attributes of God*, 133

Collins, Anthony, 83, 91

Conscience, 144

Contingence, concept of, 89-90

Cooper, Samuel, 30

Creation, Edwards on, 69-70

Cutler, Timothy, 8, 12

D

Dana, James, 149

Deism, 91, 99-100, 145, 156-57

Deism Revealed (Skelton), 152-53

Descartes, 8

Determinism, 81-83, 108-19

"Dissertation concerning the End for which God created the World, A" (Edwards), 57, 131